Favell Lee Mortimer

Apostles preaching to Jews and Gentiles

The acts explained to children

Favell Lee Mortimer

Apostles preaching to Jews and Gentiles
The acts explained to children

ISBN/EAN: 9783337136147

Printed in Europe, USA, Canada, Australia, Japan

Cover: Foto ©Lupo / pixelio.de

More available books at **www.hansebooks.com**

APOSTLES

PREACHING TO JEWS AND GENTILES

OR

The Acts

EXPLAINED TO CHILDREN.

BY THE
AUTHOR OF 'PEEP OF DAY,' &c.

'And He commanded us to preach unto the people.'—*Acts*, x. 42.

Twenty-fourth Thousand.

LONDON:
HATCHARDS, PICCADILLY.
1888.

PREFACE.

It is now full forty years since I began to write for the little ones. Again I call to the little ones, and say, 'You are the children of those for whom I first wrote, so I must call you my grand-children.' I have written to you about Peter, when he was old and fed the lambs. Also I have written about Paul the aged, who was not one of the Twelve Apostles, but who loved Jesus as much as any, or even more; for to him was much forgiven.

There are now ten books about

Jesus and His Prophets and His Apostles written by me, and I wish to say a word to your parents about which should be read *first* and which *last*.

This is the order proposed by me :—

1. *Peep of Day.*

2. *Streaks of Light,* as relating chiefly to the same events as in *Peep of Day*; somewhat amplified and adorned by exquisite hymns, selected from numerous poets.

3 and 4. *Line upon Line,* as making the child acquainted with the outline of Old Testament history.

5. *Precept upon Precept;* or, a fuller explanation of the Gospels than that contained in the two volumes which opened the series.

6. *Apostles Preaching to Jews and Gentiles.* This first introduces the child to the scenes when the Gentiles were converted under the power of the Spirit.

7. *Lines Left Out;* wherein the various miscellaneous histories and the book of Judges are explained. The earlier facts explained in *Line upon Line* might be selected and intermixed with these new facts.

8. *The Kings of Israel and Judah.* This book is joined to the former by the narrow isthmus of the histories of Saul and David. The principal parts of the histories of those two kings might now be read from the Bible.

9. *The Captivity.* The history of Judah during the seventy years of their captivity, and how at last they went back and rebuilt Jerusalem.

10. *More about Jesus.* Here facts are brought before the child,—facts with which he is acquainted, but which require to be impressed upon his heart.

If you will still listen to my voice,

let me add a few words upon the method of reading these books.

The Peep of Day should be simply read to the child.

Streaks of Light should also be read to the child or by him; but afterwards (when the child is old enough), immediately after reading each section, the child itself might read the Scripture whence each is taken.

In all the remaining books of the series this system might be pursued.

If children are old enough to read *Line upon Line* themselves, they would like to read the Scriptures *next day.*

It is very important not to tire children by letting them read too much at a time.

When the chapter in the book is

long, let it be divided; and let the same be done with the Scriptures, as much as ever the case may need.

How important that the outline of truth be engraved upon the infant mind! A time is coming which will deceive many. It behoves all mothers and grandmothers to act the part of Eunice and Lois, and to instruct the children in the Holy Scriptures, able to make them wise unto salvation through faith which is in Jesus, and able also to preserve them in the last perilous days from the evil men and seducers who will then abound.

TO THE DEAR CHILDREN WHO READ THIS BOOK.

Your grandmamma told you that she should soon leave you. She longed to go to her Saviour. Her wish has been granted. Very gently she fell asleep on the 22nd of last August. But in her books she will still speak to you, as she has done for so many years. She has also left me some true stories for you, which I hope you may have next Christmas.

L. C. M.

Trowbridge Rectory,
   Feb. 1879.

CONTENTS.

		PAGE
1.	THE TWELFTH APOSTLE	1
2.	THE PROMISED GIFT	6
3.	THE CRIPPLE	10
4.	THE FIRST IMPRISONMENT	15
5.	THE TWO LIARS	20
6.	THE SECOND IMPRISONMENT	28
7.	THE SEVEN DEACONS	33
8.	THE FIRST MARTYR	35
9.	THE FIRST MISSIONARY AFTER THE ASCENSION	42
10.	SIMON THE SORCERER	48
11.	THE HUMBLE LORD	53
12.	THE HEAVENLY VOICE	59
13.	THE COMFORTING DREAM	64
14.	THE ESCAPE IN A BASKET	67
15.	SAUL'S VISIT TO PETER	72
16.	THE WARNING DREAM	74
17.	THE CHARITABLE WOMAN	79
18.	THE VISION ON THE HOUSETOP	88
19.	PETER'S VISIT TO CORNELIUS	92
20.	PETER'S DELIVERANCE	97

CONTENTS.

		PAGE
21.	THE DEATH OF THE THIRD HEROD	105
22.	THE CHRISTIANS OF ANTIOCH	109
23.	PAUL'S FIRST MISSIONARY JOURNEY	111
24.	THE UNFAITHFUL COMPANION	118
25.	THE STONING	123
26.	PAUL'S SHORT JOURNEY TO JERUSALEM	130
27.	PAUL'S SECOND MISSIONARY JOURNEY	136
28.	THE WOMAN FULL OF PRAYERS	141
29.	THE STRIPES	147
30.	THE EARTHQUAKE	153
31.	PAUL SET FREE	159
32.	PAUL AT THESSALONICA	165
33.	PAUL AT BEREA	169
34.	PAUL AT ATHENS	173
35.	PAUL AT CORINTH	176
36.	END OF PAUL'S SECOND MISSIONARY JOURNEY	182
37.	THE ELOQUENT PREACHER	188
38.	PAUL'S THIRD MISSIONARY JOURNEY	191
39.	THE DISCIPLES OF JOHN THE BAPTIST AT EPHESUS	195
40.	PAUL'S MEETING WITH APOLLOS	199
41.	THE SORCERERS	202
42.	THE UPROAR AT EPHESUS	205
43.	THE COMING OF TITUS	209
44.	THE SLEEPY HEARER	212
45.	PAUL'S FAREWELL TO THE EPHESIANS	216
46.	PAUL'S VISIT TO PHILIP	221
47.	JOY IN JERUSALEM	227

CONTENTS.

		PAGE
48.	THE UPROAR IN THE TEMPLE	230
49.	THE UPROAR ON THE CASTLE STAIRS	234
50.	PAUL'S ESCAPE FROM SCOURGING	239
51.	A JOYFUL NIGHT IN THE CASTLE	242
52.	THE PLOT DISCOVERED	246
53.	THE JOURNEY TO CÆSAREA	249
54.	THE PRISON AT CÆSAREA	253
55.	THE TREMBLING JUDGE	258
56.	THE DISAPPOINTMENT OF THE JEWS	264
57.	KING AGRIPPA'S VISIT	269
58.	THE BEGINNING OF THE VOYAGE	275
59.	THE STORM AT SEA	280
60.	THE LAST NIGHT OF THE VOYAGE	283
61.	THE SHIPWRECK	287
62.	THE VIPER	291
63.	LANDING IN ITALY	296
64.	ARRIVAL AT ROME	300
65.	PAUL'S FRIENDS AND VISITORS AT ROME	306
66.	THE GLORIOUS VISIONS OF JOHN	316

QUESTIONS TO BE ASKED AFTER READING EACH CHAPTER 321

LIST OF ILLUSTRATIONS.

	PAGE
HEALING THE SICK IN THE STREETS OF JERUSALEM	*Frontispiece.*
PETER AND JOHN HEALING THE LAME MAN	12
ANANIAS AND SAPPHIRA CONCEALING THE MONEY	22
THE DEATH OF SAPPHIRA	26
THE STONING OF STEPHEN	39
SAUL PERSECUTING THE CHRISTIANS	43
PETER REBUKING SIMON THE SORCERER	51
SAUL'S MIRACULOUS CONVERSION	61
THE HEALING OF ÆNEAS BY PETER	81
THE WIDOWS EXHIBITING THE WORK OF DORCAS	85
RHODA AT THE GATE	102
ELYMAS THE SORCERER STRUCK BLIND	115
PAUL HEALING A POOR CRIPPLE	126
PAUL'S RECOVERY AFTER HAVING BEEN STONED	131
SEPARATION OF PAUL AND BARNABAS	137

	PAGE
LYDIA'S INVITATION TO PAUL AND HIS COMPANIONS	145
PAUL AND THE SORCERESS	149
THE PHILIPPIAN JAILER	156
THE JUDGES RELEASING PAUL AND SILAS	162
EUTYCHUS RESTORED	214
PAUL'S FAREWELL TO THE EPHESIANS	219
PAUL'S FAREWELL TO THE CHRISTIANS OF TYRE	223
PAUL ADDRESSING THE JEWS FROM THE CASTLE STAIRS	236
FELIX TREMBLING BEFORE PAUL	261
PAUL'S DEFENCE BEFORE AGRIPPA	273
PAUL SHAKING OFF THE VIPER	294
PAUL WITH HIS FRIENDS AT ROME	303

APOSTLES PREACHING TO JEWS AND GENTILES.

I.

THE TWELFTH APOSTLE.

Acts, i. 12 to end.

Do you not wish to know what the Apostles did after Jesus went up to heaven?

We know what they did; for a history has been written called the Acts of the Apostles.

It was Luke who wrote that history—the same Luke who wrote the history of Jesus called the Gospel of Luke. Luke was not one of the twelve apostles, but he knew a great deal about Jesus and His twelve apostles, and the Holy Spirit taught him what to write.

You know there were eleven apostles, who saw Jesus caught up to heaven. Two angels stood near, and comforted them by saying, 'This same Jesus, which is taken up from you into heaven, shall so come in like manner as ye have seen Him go into heaven.'

This sweet promise made them very joyful.

It was on Mount Olivet they were standing when Jesus was taken up out of their sight. They had only a mile to go to Jerusalem. They went there and stayed there.

Why did they stay there? There were many in Jerusalem who hated them, and who wished to kill them. The priests and Pharisees were there who had killed Jesus. Why, then, did the apostles remain in that city?

Because Jesus had bid them wait in

Jerusalem till He should send down the Holy Ghost.

They used often to meet together in a large room upstairs, and they used to pray very earnestly for the Holy Ghost. There were many more than the eleven apostles who met together. Mary, the mother of Jesus, came there, and other women who loved Jesus, and who once went to His tomb. (You know their names.) And there were the brethren of Jesus, and many other holy men, who lived in this room. Altogether there were one hundred and twenty people.

One day Peter stood up among the believers in this room, and made a short speech. What was it about? It was about choosing another apostle in the place of Judas, so as to make up the number of the twelve again. Peter had read in the Psalms,—'Let another take his office.'* He knew that verse was about

---

* The word translated 'office' in Ps. cix. 8, is translated 'bishopric' in Peter's speech, and means 'apostleship.'

Judas. It was the office of Judas to be an apostle, and God said that another man should be an apostle instead, and so take his office.

'You know,' said Peter, 'that a field was bought with the money that Judas got for selling his Lord, and you know that in this field he fell down, and that his body burst* in the midst, so that the field is called "The field of blood." God has said, "Let another take his office." Let us now fix on a man to be in the place of Judas.' Peter knew it must be a man who had known Jesus well when He was on earth, and could tell people about His rising from the grave.

There were two men in the room that had known Jesus a long while. Their names were Joseph Justus and Matthias. Peter thought either of them fit to be an apostle, and he did not know which to choose. So Peter and

* Judas probably got on a tree overhanging some place in the field and there hanged himself, and the rope or the branch broke.

the rest of the apostles prayed to God to let them know which He had chosen.

How did they expect God to answer their prayer? Did God speak? Did an angel come? No!

The apostles cast lots.

There are many ways of casting lots. Perhaps the apostles cast lots in this way. Perhaps they wrote the name of Joseph Justus on one little piece of wood called a tablet, and the name of Matthias on another, and then shook these two tablets in the end of a robe, till one tablet fell out. The tablet that fell out had the name of Matthias written on it. It was a great honour to be one of the twelve apostles. Yet we never hear again of Matthias. But he will sit on one of the twelve thrones that Jesus promised to His apostles.

'The lot is cast into the lap: but the whole disposing thereof is of the Lord.'—*Prov.* xvi. 33.

II.

THE PROMISED GIFT.
Acts, ii. 1–15, 22–24, 32–38.

Ten days had now passed away since Jesus had gone up to heaven. How long did Jesus spend on earth after He had risen? Forty days. Ten more days make fifty days.

It was now fifty days since Jesus rose. There was a feast of the Jews at that time, called 'the feast of first-fruits,' when the Jews brought their first sheaves of wheat to present to the Lord. Thousands of Jews came up from all countries to keep this feast. One name for the feast was Pentecost.* It was now just fifty days after the Passover. It was the first day of the week. On that day the believers in Jesus met together in the large room to pray.

* *Pento* means five. *Pentecost* means fiftieth.

THE PROMISED GIFT.

It was early in the morning—about eight o'clock. Suddenly a great sound was heard. It was like the sound of a very strong, high wind. This great sound filled the place where the believers were sitting, and shook the whole house. There came also what looked like fire—divided into many parts, each part appearing to be a tongue of fire; and these came and sat on each of the believers,—on the women as well as on the men. At the same time they all were able to speak many strange languages which they had never learned. Jesus had once told His apostles to preach the Gospel to every creature, and they may have wondered how they should be able to teach strange nations; but now they were made able to speak to every one in his own language.

The great noise which had shaken the house had been heard in all Jerusalem, and people came running towards the place. They could not all get into the house, but the people in the house could come out to the people in the street. The bright tongues were still to be seen upon them. There were Jews who lived in other countries, as well as Gentiles, and they heard the believers speaking in the languages they spoke in the countries where they were born. They were very much astonished, and said, 'How do these men of Galilee speak all these languages?' Some thought this was a miracle, and said to each other, 'What is the meaning of it?' But others only mocked, and said, 'These men have drunk too much wine.'

Then Peter stood up, and all the other apostles stood near him. He spake in a very loud voice, that all the multitude might hear.

He began by saying,—' These men are not drunken, as you suppose; for men do not get drunk so early in the morning. But,' said he, 'God has sent down His Holy Spirit, as He promised. Hear my words,' cried out Peter; 'Jesus of Nazareth, who did so many miracles among you, as you know, has been crucified by your wicked hands. But He has been raised from the dead, and taken to God's right hand, and now He hath sent forth THIS which ye now SEE and hear.'

The multitude could see the brightness of the Spirit. Many now believed that Jesus was the Son of God, and felt very unhappy for having crucified Him; and they were pricked in their hearts, and came to the apostles, saying very sorrowfully, 'What shall we do?'

Then Peter answered, 'Repent and be baptized every one of you in the name of Jesus, for the forgiveness of your sins, and you shall receive the Holy Ghost.'

Three thousand were baptized that day.

Then was fulfilled what John the

Baptist once said: 'I indeed baptize you with water unto repentance, but He that cometh after me shall baptize you with the Holy Ghost and with FIRE.'—Matt. iii. 11.

III.

THE CRIPPLE.

Acts, ii. 41 to end; iii. 1–19.

THE three thousand people who believed lived very happily. They went often to see each other, and they all loved one another, and they prayed together.

Some were very poor and some were very rich. Those who were rich sold their fine houses and gardens, and with the money they helped the poor people.

The apostles did a great many miracles.

Let us hear the account of one of these miracles.

Acts, iii. 6.

'Then Peter said, Silver and gold have I none; but such as I have give I thee: In the name of Jesus Christ of Nazareth rise up and walk.'

Peter and John went up to the Temple one afternoon, about three o'clock, when the lamb was sacrificed on the altar. As they passed through a fine brass gate called Beautiful, they saw a poor beggar lying there. He was lame. He had been born with weak bones in his ankles and feet, so that he could never walk. He was now forty years old, and he had no hope of ever being cured. Every day his friends carried him to this gate, that he might beg money of the people passing through. In the evening his friends carried him home.

When he saw Peter and John coming through, he begged them to give him something. Peter and John stopped, and said to the beggar, 'Fix your eyes on us.' So the man looked, in great hopes of a little money. Then Peter said, 'Silver and gold have I none, but such as I have give I thee: In the name of Jesus of Nazareth rise up and walk.' Then Peter took the beggar by his right hand, and helped him to get up. But the man sprang from the ground with a leap, though before he could not stand; but his feet and ankle-bones had been made strong in a moment.

The man followed Peter and John into the Temple, leaping as he went, and praising God. There were a great many people in the courts of the Temple who had come up to pray, and they saw the man leaping, and they knew him well as the beggar who had sat at the gate year after year.

The man was so fond of Peter and John that he held them fast, lest they should go away. People in the streets heard what had happened, and came in crowds to see the man. They looked at Peter and John, admiring them, and thinking they were very great men to do such a wonder.

But Peter and John did not want

to be admired. They wanted everybody to praise the Saviour. So Peter stood up to preach in the Temple courts. He said, 'Ye men of Israel, why do you look on us, as though by our own power and goodness we had made this man walk? It is through believing on Jesus he was cured. You asked Pontius Pilate to have Jesus killed, and to let go the murderer Barabbas. But God raised Him from the dead, and took Him up to heaven, where He will stay till the happy time that God has spoken of. Repent ye, therefore, and be converted, that your sins may be blotted out.'

IV.

THE FIRST IMPRISONMENT.

Acts, iv. 1–31.

PETER had just preached his second sermon written in the Bible. He had preached it in the *Temple.* His first sermon was preached in the *street*,—*this*—in the Temple. There were more enemies here in the Temple than there had been in the street, for the priests were here who hated Jesus, and could not bear to hear that He was still alive, having risen from the grave. A whole troop of them came, seized Peter and John, and put them in a prison close by. They could not judge them that evening, for it was getting dark.

What a dreadful thing to spend a night in prison—a close, unpleasant, dark dungeon! This was the first night that the apostles were imprisoned, but it was not the *last*.

The judges were called the Sanhedrim. There were about seventy of them. Their hall of judgment was close to the Temple. Early in the morning Peter and John were taken out of prison and made to stand before the judges. These judges sat in a half-circle round the wall. Amongst them

THE FIRST IMPRISONMENT. 17

was Christ's great enemy—Caiaphas, the High Priest.

But Nicodemus and Joseph of Arimathea were not there, though they belonged to the Sanhedrim.

Many of the relations of Caiaphas came to see the judgment.

But who is that man standing by Peter and John, looking so loving and so brave? He is a very poor man, yet joy is in his looks. It is the poor cripple who sat at the gate yesterday begging.

Looking towards this man, the judges said to Peter and John, 'By what name, or by what power, have you done *this?*' That is to say, *How* have you cured that lame man?

Then Peter was filled with the Holy Ghost, and answered boldly: 'By the name of Jesus Christ of Nazareth, whom ye crucified, whom God raised from the dead, even by *Him* doth this man stand before you quite well.'

Then he added these words, 'There

is none other name under heaven given among men, whereby we must be saved.' It is not only *that* poor cripple is saved from his lameness by Jesus, but that same precious Name can save us from hell and death, and no other name can do it.

The judges were surprised to hear Peter speak so boldly for his Master.

But though the judges saw that a great miracle had been done, they were determined not to believe in Jesus themselves and to prevent other people believing. This was the sin against the Holy Ghost. When you yourself believe and yet try to prevent others believing, that is the sin against the Holy Ghost, as when the Pharisees *saw* the miracles of Jesus and said He did them through Satan, to prevent others believing on Him. This is the sin that cannot be forgiven. The priests did just the same now. They forbade Peter and John to teach any more.

The judges would have liked to punish Peter and John; but as the people saw the very man who had been cured standing before their eyes, the judges were afraid to punish the apostles. All they could do was to command them not to teach or to preach in the name of Jesus any more.

But Peter and John boldly answered, ' Is it right in the sight of God to obey *you* sooner than God ?'

God had told them to speak, and they said they would speak. How gladly now would the judges have killed them ! but they were afraid of making the people angry, and so they let them go.

Peter and John hastened home to their own friends, and told them all that happened to them during the night and in the morning. And then they prayed together, and thanked God for doing wonders in the name of Jesus. As soon as they had done praying the house was shaken by the Holy Ghost entering in once more and making them speak boldly about Jesus.

The words of Jesus to His apostles before He was crucified:—
'If the world hate you, you know that it hated me before it hated you.'—*John*, xv. 18.

V.

THE TWO LIARS.

Acts, iv. 32 to end ; v. 1-11.

There were now a great many people who believed in Jesus. Three thousand had turned to Him after Peter's *first* sermon on the morning of Pentecost, and five thousand more had turned after Peter's second sermon in the Temple one evening. Three thousand and five thousand made eight thousand.

ACTS, v. 2.
'And kept back part of the price, his wife also being privy to it.'

They lived very happily, sharing their things with one another. The rich sold their lands, and gave the money to the poor.

One rich man, named Barnabas, sold his land, and brought the money to the apostles, and laid it at their feet, to do what they would with it. You will often hear again of this good Barnabas.

But were all the believers good? No; there were some who did not believe with their *hearts*. They wished to go to heaven, but they did not love Jesus: they tried to seem good, and to get praised.

There was a rich man, named Ananias, who wanted to be praised. He had a wife named Sapphira. They thought they would like to seem as good as Barnabas, but they did not like to part with all their money. One said to the other, 'Let us sell our land, and give the price to the apostles—but not quite *all*. Oh, then we shall not seem so good as Barnabas. Cannot we *pretend* to give it all ? The apostles will never know what money we got for the land, and we will let them think we have given them the *whole* for the poor.'

So Ananias took *part* of the money, and took it to the apostles, and laid it at their feet, and hoped they would think he had given all.

Did the apostles know ? You will see by what Peter said,—

'Why has Satan filled your heart to lie to the Holy Ghost, and to keep back *part* of the price of the land? You need not have sold the land at all, and when you had sold it you need not have brought us the money. Why have you thought in your heart of doing this ?' (You see that it is sin in the *heart* that God hates.)

As soon as Ananias heard Peter's words he fell down dead. Some young

ACTS, v. 10.
'Then fell she down straightway at his feet, and yielded up the ghost.'

men took up his body, wrapped round it linen cloths, and took it out and buried it. Every one who heard of this sudden death was filled with fear.

But Sapphira did not hear of it, so she was not frightened. About three hours after her husband's death she came in — perhaps expecting to be thanked and praised. Then Peter tried her, to see whether she joined in the lie. He said,—'How much did you sell the land for?' She said they had sold it for the sum that Ananias had brought to the apostles, though they had really sold it for more.

Peter replied,—'Why did you agree together to tempt the Spirit of the Lord? Behold, the feet of those which have buried thy husband shall carry thee out.'

Immediately Sapphira fell down dead, and the young men who were returned from burying her husband buried her also. The people who had been frightened at hearing of Ananias' death were still more frightened now.

Many children have been made afraid to tell lies by hearing of these dreadful deaths. There is also this terrible verse to make them fear God's everlasting anger :—

'All liars shall have their part in the lake which burneth with fire and brimstone.'—*Rev.* xxi. 8.

VI.

THE SECOND IMPRISONMENT.
Acts, v. 12 to end.

AFTER the sudden death of Ananias and Sapphira, people honoured the apostles more than ever. They brought numbers of their sick friends to be cured. They placed them in the streets on their beds, that if Peter should pass by his shadow falling on them might heal them. People came from all the cities round about Jerusalem, and the sick were healed and the devils cast out. What did these miracles show? They showed that what the apostles said of Peter's Master was all true, and that He was really the Son of God.

The high priest and his friends could not bear to hear the apostles praised, and they sent men to seize them and take them to prison. The prison was the place where thieves and murderers were shut up. What a place for holy men to spend the night!

We do not know how many of the apostles were shut up this time. But they did not spend the whole night there, for an angel came in the darkness, and unlocked the prison doors so quietly that the soldiers, watching all around, never heard him come. The soldiers did not even see the apostles go out, therefore it seems certain that God had made them all sleep soundly that night, though they ought to have been awake.

The angel, after leading the apostles out, said, in parting,—'Go, speak in the Temple all the words of this life.'

So as soon as it was light they went to the Temple, and began to preach as usual. Perhaps they may have had time to go home first to refresh their weary bodies, and to see their weeping friends.

But the high priest knew nothing about what had happened that night, neither did the other judges.

Early in the morning they all met together in the great hall, called the Sanhedrim. A great many judges were in the hall that day. They were very anxious to see the apostles, and they sent men to the prison to fetch them. But the men came back, saying, 'We cannot find the prisoners. We found the prison all locked up, and the keepers standing before the gates, but when we opened the doors we could not find any one.'

The judges were very much astonished to hear this, and they could not think what had become of the apostles, till a man came in and said,—' Behold, the men whom you put in prison are standing in the Temple, teaching the people!' Here was another surprise. The priests had never thought that the apostles would go on teaching after having been put in prison. Of course, they felt very angry, but the soldiers, who fetched them, were obliged to bring the apostles gently, or the people might have stoned the soldiers.

When they were brought, and standing before the judges, the high priest asked them,—' Did not we command you *not* to teach in this name? And behold, you have taught all the people in Jerusalem; and you want to make us guilty of killing this man!'

He did not like to mention the name of Jesus, so he called Him 'this man.'

Peter and the other apostles answered, 'We ought to obey God rather than men. God hath raised up Jesus, whom you killed and hanged upon a tree.'

The judges grew more angry than ever, and wanted to kill the apostles. But there was a wise man amongst them, named Gamaliel, who sent the apostles out for a little while; then he advised the other judges not to punish the apostles, lest they should really be God's people. So the rest agreed to let them go, after they had beaten them first. But the apostles did not mind the beating, and went away rejoicing that they were counted worthy to suffer shame for His name.

'And daily in the Temple, and in every house, they ceased not to teach and preach Jesus Christ.' —*Acts*, v. 42.

VII.

THE SEVEN DEACONS.
Acts, vi. 1–7.

THERE were now thousands and thousands of believers in Jesus. Amongst them were many poor widows. The apostles had a great deal of money that rich people had given them for the poor. They spent some of this money in buying food for the poor widows, and they gave them a portion every day.

This was a great deal of trouble, and took up a great deal of time. Yet the apostles could not satisfy all the widows. Some of these widows belonged to Jerusalem, and spoke Hebrew; others came from distant lands, and these widows spoke Greek. It was these Greek-speaking widows who grew discontented. Some of their friends took their part, and said they had not their right share of food daily.

When the apostles heard what was said, they called the brethren together to propose a plan to them.

They said, ' *We* cannot look after giving food to all these widows, because we must continually pray and preach the word. So you had better choose seven good men to give out the food.'

The multitude of believers liked this plan, and chose seven men who were known to be very good. The chief of the seven was named Stephen. He was indeed a holy and a wise man, and you will hear much about him. There was another named Philip. You will hear something more of him, but of the rest you will never hear anything.

All these seven men were to be called deacons, or servants, for they were to help the apostles to serve. There was an *apostle* named Philip, and now there was a *deacon* Philip also. The apostles prayed over these seven deacons, and laid their hands on them to give them the power of doing miracles.

Soon afterwards a great many of the priests believed on Jesus: to persuade the priests to believe was a wonder indeed, such as Christ had promised His apostles they should do through faith in His name, after He was gone up on high.

'Verily, verily, I say unto you, He that believeth on me, the works that I do shall he do also; and *greater* works than these shall he do, because I go unto my Father.'—*John*, xiv. 12.

VIII.

THE FIRST MARTYR.

Acts, vi. 7 to end.

STEPHEN was the most remarkable of all the seven deacons. He was full of faith, and did great wonders among the people.

But the enemies of Jesus hated him the more for being so wonderful. Learned Jews went to him and disputed with him, but they found that Stephen was wiser than they were.

So they determined to bring him before the great council, called the Sanhedrim, and to bribe men to tell lies of him. And they went about among the people and tried to set the people against him, by saying false things of him.

One day they came suddenly upon him and caught him, and brought him to the great hall of the Sanhedrim, close to the Temple, and set him before his judges.

False witnesses came in and said that Stephen had declared that Jesus of Nazareth would destroy the Temple. Stephen had never said this, for it would be the Romans who would destroy the Temple.

After Stephen had been so falsely accused, the judges, who sat round, looked at him, and were surprised to see his face like the face of an angel, so bright,—so glorious,—so holy. But this sight did not turn the hearts of the wicked judges. They went on judging him.

The high priest was the chief among them. (It was not Caiaphas now who was high priest. He had been put out of his place.)

This high priest, after hearing the wicked men accuse him, said to Stephen, 'Are these things so?'

Then Stephen began to defend himself against what the false witnesses had said of him. He made a very long speech; at last he told his judges that all of them had been murderers of the Son of God.

This made the judges very angry. Stephen's words cut them to the heart, but did not make them repent. 'They gnashed upon him with their teeth.' They were like devils,—he,—like an angel.

He lifted up his eyes towards heaven and saw there the glory of God, and Jesus standing on His right hand.

Then he cried out, 'Behold, I see the heavens opened, and Jesus standing on the right hand of God!'

Then they cried out with a loud voice, and stopped their ears, that they might not hear Stephen's blessed words, and they ran upon him all together (as the men of Nazareth had once hunted Jesus). They ran far from the Temple courts, all along the street that led to a gate of the city, near the brook Kedron; and when they had got Stephen out, they took up great stones and threw them at him.

In order to hurl the stones with more force they took off their outer garments, and asked a young man named Saul to take care of them. He was an unbelieving young man, who was glad to see Stephen killed.

Stephen went on praying all the time the stones were falling, calling

ACTS, VII. 59.
'And they stoned Stephen, calling upon God, and saying, Lord Jesus, receive my spirit.'

out, 'Lord Jesus, receive my spirit.' At last, when bruised all over and ready to die, he kneeled down and said, 'Lord, lay not this sin to their charge!' Thus with his last breath he asked God to forgive his cruel murderers.

As soon as he had offered this prayer he fell asleep.

This was the death of the first martyr. Thousands and thousands of martyrs have died like him, praising God and praying for their enemies, and they will all come with Jesus to reign with Him in glory.

The host of martyrs :—

'And they overcame him by the blood of the Lamb, and by the word of their testimony; and they loved not their lives unto the death.'—*Rev.* xii. 11.

IX.

THE FIRST MISSIONARY AFTER THE ASCENSION.

Acts, viii. 1–13.

The dead body of Stephen was not left to be cast out by his enemies. It was buried by holy men, with tears and sighs.

The Jews went on ill-treating the believers at Jerusalem; so that many of them went to other cities to get out of the reach of their enemies. Saul, that young man, who kept the clothes of the stoners, was the fiercest of all. He went into any house he pleased, and dragged the believers to prison—both men and women.

But the apostles would not leave Jerusalem. They went on preaching pardon to the murderers of Jesus, if they would repent.

One of the deacons was named Philip.

ACTS, VIII. 3.

'As for Saul, he made havoc of the church, entering into every house, and haling men and women, committed them to prison.'

He went down to Samaria to preach. He did not go to Sychar, in Samaria, where Jesus had once preached to the woman at the well. He went to the finest city in Samaria. Its name was the same as the name of the country—Samaria. It was built on a beautiful hill, that rises up in the midst of a sweet and fruitful valley. This city was a very wicked place. There were idol temples in it, and there were men who worshipped Satan himself. Here Philip preached about Jesus; and he also did many great miracles, for the apostles had once laid their hands on him, and given this power to him as well as to Stephen. Many unclean spirits and devils came out of poor creatures when Philip commanded them. Helpless creatures with the palsy rose up and walked at Philip's word, and lame people leaped like stags.

When men saw what wonders Philip could do they believed what he told them about Jesus, and there was great joy in all the city. Why? Because they knew Christ and His salvation.

Amongst the men who believed there was one more wicked than the rest. His name was Simon. He had been a great deceiver, and had made people believe he was very great, so that everybody said,—'This man is the great power of God.' Little children said so, and old men said so, too : rich and poor—all admired and praised Simon. He was called a sorcerer. What is that? A man who trusts in Satan, and gets help from him ; a man who tells lies, and plays all kinds of deceitful tricks.

But now this wicked Simon believed what Philip said, and he asked to be baptized. People no longer thought him wonderful.

Every one listened to Philip, and wondered at his miracles. Philip thought that Simon was turned from his wickedness, and that he believed in Jesus with his heart. So he baptized him. But Simon's heart was not changed.

You know Christ once said, 'Except a man be born of water and of the Spirit, he cannot enter into the kingdom of God' (John, iii. 5). Simon was baptized, and he was born of water, but he was not born of the Spirit. He was just as wicked as ever. 'Though he believed that Jesus was the Son of God, he did not love Him.' He stood by Philip, wondering at his miracles, and sorry that he himself could no longer do the wonderful things that he had once done when he was a great sorcerer. He did not repent of his past wickedness, nor pray to Christ for pardon.

'Now if any man have not the Spirit of Christ, he is none of His.'—*Rom.* viii. 9.

X.

SIMON THE SORCERER.

Acts, viii. 14-24.

THE apostles, you remember, remained at Jerusalem. They were not afraid of the cruel hatred of the Jews. They heard the good news, that the city of Samaria was full of believers. They thought that they could do them good by coming to see them.

So the apostles sent Peter and John down to Samaria. These two apostles were such friends that they generally went together.

When they came to Samaria they found a great many men and women who had turned to God, and who had been baptized by Philip. But they found none who could do miracles by the Holy Ghost.

So Peter and John laid their hands on the heads of the believers, and prayed that God would give them the Holy Ghost.

Philip had not laid his hands on the believers, for he was not an apostle; he was only a deacon, and he could not bestow the gift of the Holy Ghost on other people. None but the apostles could do this.

When Simon saw what the apostles did to the believers, he thought he should like to be able to do the same, that he might be admired, as he used to be, and that he might get rich. So he took some money, and offered it to Peter and John, and said,—'Do give me this power, that when I lay my hands on any one he may receive the Holy Ghost.'

The apostles were much displeased at Simon thinking they would take money for the gift of God. They were grieved at his having such a wicked thought in his heart. Peter said to him,—'Thy money perish as well as thou, because thou hast THOUGHT that the gift of God may be bought with money. Thy heart is not right in the sight of God. Repent of thy wickedness, and pray God, if perhaps the *thought* of thy heart may be forgiven thee. I see that thou art in the chains of sin.'

Simon seemed frightened by Peter's answer, for he said,—'Pray to the Lord for me, that nothing you have said may come to me.' You see he did not ask to be forgiven, but only not to be punished. This was the sign that his heart was not right.

He had never really turned to God. He still wanted to get money, and to be praised by men for his power. He was like the two liars—Ananias and Sapphira—a hypocrite. He was like Judas—a devil; and he had the curse of God upon him.* His money was to perish, and he was to perish. Oh, how

* 'He that committeth sin is of the devil, for the devil sinneth from the beginning.'—1 *John*, iii. 8.

ACTS, VIII. 20.

'But Peter said unto him, Thy money perish with thee, because thou hast thought that the gift of God may be purchased with money.'

terrible it is only to pretend to turn to God, and not to turn with all the heart!

XI.

THE HUMBLE LORD.

Acts, viii. 26 to end.

THE apostles Peter and John soon left Samaria and returned to Jerusalem. They preached in many villages by the way. Perhaps they went to Sychar once more, and saw that woman who once stood by the well with Jesus.

Philip also did not remain in Samaria, but he did not return to Jerusalem.

God had a great work for Philip to do. He was to bring the Gospel into Africa. There were then three parts of the world. Asia, where Jesus had preached; Europe, where we live, and where the Gospel had not yet been preached; and Africa, where black people lived. To Africa—God determined to send the Gospel.

The angel told Philip to go down to the Philistines' country, at the lower corner of Canaan. Gaza was in that part, but Philip did not go near that town; he went to a desert place near it, on the way to Africa.

It must have seemed strange to Philip to hear he must go to a desert. He might wonder whom he could preach to in a desert. But he went. While he was walking among the rocky hills he saw a very fine carriage going along. It was coming from Jerusalem. There were horses and servants. A great lord was sitting in the carriage reading. This great lord was the chief servant of a great queen called Candace. She was the queen of a hot country in Africa called Ethiopia, where the people are almost black.

This lord had the charge of all the queen's treasure, and he was called her treasurer. But we do not know his name.

The Spirit said to Philip, 'Go near to that chariot;' and Philip went. He heard the treasurer reading out loud. He had a scroll, and not a book, in his hand. On that scroll, or roll, were written the words of the prophet Isaiah.

Who would have thought that a lord from a heathen country would read the Word of God?

But this man had been up to Jerusalem to worship in the Temple. He had not been allowed to go further than the outer court of the Gentiles, but his prayers in that court were heard, as much as the prayers of the priests in the Holy Place. He had brought back a greater treasure than all his gold and silver, even the words that God once spoke to Isaiah.

Philip had the courage to speak to this great lord. He said to him, 'Do you understand what you are reading?'

If the treasurer had been a proud man he would have been affronted by that question from a poor stranger; but he was humble, and he answered: 'How can I understand if I have no one to teach me?' And then he asked Philip to come and sit by him in his chariot. When Philip was sitting in the chariot, the rich man showed him what he was reading. It was that sweet verse in the fifty-third chapter: 'He is brought as a lamb to the slaughter, and as a sheep before her shearers is dumb, so he openeth not his mouth.'

The treasurer, after having read this verse, said to Philip, 'I do not know the meaning of this. Does the Prophet speak of himself, or of some other man?'

Then Philip explained it all to him. He told him that Jesus was the lamb, and that He had lately been crucified in Jerusalem; and that He had been as meek to His enemies as a sheep who makes no noise when he is sheared. And he told him that Jesus had risen from His grave, and that He had desired His disciples to go and teach people of all countries, and to baptize them in His name.

The treasurer listened very attentively, and wanted to know whether he might be baptized. Just at this moment the chariot passed by a stream. There are not many streams in the desert, and the treasurer was pleased to see water. He cried out, ' Here is water ; may I not be baptized ?'

Philip said, ' You may, if you believe with all your heart.'

The treasurer replied, 'I believe that Jesus Christ is the Son of God.'

When Philip saw that he believed he desired the driver to stop the horses; and Philip and the treasurer both got out and went together into the water. There Philip baptized this Gentile stranger

As soon as they were come up out of the water the Spirit caught up Philip, and took him to a place by the seaside. He took him in the air in a wonderful manner.

The place where the Spirit left him was once called Ashdod. It was a place full of idols. Philip went along by the seaside, from place to place, preaching everywhere. At last he stopped at a fine city called Cæsarea, built by the Roman Emperor, and called after Cæsar.

The treasurer must have been sorry to lose his teacher, yet he was so happy in his Saviour that he went to his home full of joy, ready to teach the Queen Candace and all her people. So the Gospel came into Africa, where many people turned to Jesus.

'Whosoever shall call upon the name of the Lord shall be saved.'
—*Rom.* x. 13.

XII.

THE HEAVENLY VOICE.

Acts, ix. 1-9.

A VERY wonderful event is now to be related.

You remember there was a young man named Saul, who treated cruelly the disciples of Jesus. He kept the clothes of those who stoned the holy Stephen.

This young man thought he did right in ill-treating believers in Christ, for he thought Christ was a deceiver, and not really the Son of God. After he had done much harm in Jerusalem, he went to other cities to hurt the believers who lived in them.

There was a great city, called Damascus, more than a hundred miles from Jerusalem. He wished to go there. First, he got letters from the high priest at Jerusalem, giving him leave to seize the believers in Damascus, and to bring them in chains to Jerusalem. He meant to show these letters to the chief Jews in Damascus. But on the way such an event happened!

Saul was travelling with several men as his guard. They all arrived in sight of Damascus about noonday, when the sun is the brightest. There suddenly appeared a light from heaven, brighter than the sun. This light was so dazzling that all the travellers fell down with their faces to the ground, quite unable to look up.

While thus lying prostrate, Saul heard a voice from heaven, saying,—'Saul, Saul, why dost thou persecute me?'

Saul answered,—'Who art thou, Lord?'

The voice replied,—'I am Jesus, whom thou persecutest.'

Saul, still trembling and astonished,

ACTS, IX. 7.
'And the men which journeyed with him stood speechless, hearing a voice, but seeing no man.'

inquired,—'Lord, what wouldst thou have me to do?'

The voice replied,—'Arise, and go into the city, and it shall be told thee what thou must do.'

All this time the other men did not speak a word, but they could not hear *what* Jesus said to Paul, only they heard a sound. After being struck to the ground they got up and stood by Saul, but Saul himself did not get up till Jesus said,—'Rise, and stand upon thy feet.' Then Saul arose, and opened his eyes —but behold!—he could not see— the dazzling light had blinded him. The men were not blinded, and they led Saul by the hand into the city. They took him to a lodging in Straight Street, at the house of a man named Judas. There Saul sat down, quite blind, and he refused to eat or drink for three days. As he sat in darkness he was thinking of his sins against Jesus, and of his cruelty to His people.

He felt so grieved at all he had done that he could not eat. He thought of the poor creatures he had sent to prison—of those he had beaten—and of Stephen, who had been stoned before his eyes, 'Oh, how could I be so wicked? I am the chief of sinners!'

'Christ Jesus came into the world to save sinners; of whom I am chief.'—1 *Tim.* i. 15.

XIII.

THE COMFORTING DREAM.

Acts, ix. 10-22.

WHILE Saul was in this sad state of blindness and misery—God sent him a dream. It was a comforting dream.

Saul saw a man in his dream whose name was Ananias. He came into the room, and put his hand on Saul, and said,—'Receive thy sight.' Till this dream came, how could Saul know that he should ever see again? He knew that he well deserved to be always blind. But he kept on praying to God for pardon.

While Saul was praying, there was a man in Damascus who had a dream. This man was the same Ananias that Saul had seen in his dream. He was a very good man, and he had heard that Saul was coming from Jerusalem to seize God's people, and to bind them in chains. He was much surprised when God said to him in a dream—'Get up, and go into Straight Street, and find the house of a man called Judas, and ask for a man called Saul: for Saul is now praying to me; and he has seen you in a dream coming in and putting your hand on him, that he may be able to see.'

Ananias answered the Lord,—'Many people have told me of this man, and of how much harm he has done to the holy people in Jerusalem; and how he has come here with leave from the chief priests to bind all that call on the Lord Jesus.'

But the Lord answered Ananias,— 'Go thy way, for I have chosen him to tell many people about me—Gentiles, and kings, and the children of Israel —and I shall show him that he must suffer a great deal for my sake.'

Then Ananias went to Straight Street, and entered into the house of Judas, and went up into Saul's room, and put his hands on Saul, and said, 'Brother Saul, the Lord Jesus, who appeared to you as you came to this place, has sent me to you, that you may receive your sight.' As he said this, something like skin fell from Saul's eyes, and Saul found he was able to see. Soon afterwards he was baptized, and then he ate food, and he grew strong again.

Saul stayed a good while in Damascus, and he became great friends with all the people of the Lord in the city. Those very people that he once meant to send to prison were now his dearest friends. He went to the synagogues, and preached there about Jesus Christ, that He was the Son of God.

'The Lord openeth the eyes of the blind: the Lord raiseth them that are bowed down.'—*Ps.* cxlvi. 8.

XIV.

THE ESCAPE IN A BASKET.

Gal. i. 17, 18. Acts, ix. 23-25.

AFTER Saul had been preaching a little while in Damascus, he left the city to go and live in the desert. There was a desert place very near Damascus, called Arabia. You remember that Jesus Himself went into a desert, or wilderness, for forty days, at the beginning of His preaching. Saul did the same, though he did not go into the same wilderness as Jesus did, for Jesus went into the wilderness of Judea.

Jesus in His desert was tempted of the devil; but we believe that Saul in the desert of Arabia was taught by Jesus. We think he saw His face there, and heard His voice. How happy Saul must have been in the desert,* if he met Jesus there; and we think he did, because he often tells us how he was taught everything by Jesus Christ, and nothing by man.†

But Saul might not stay long in the desert. He returned to Damascus, to

---

* Learned men believe that Saul went into the desert which extends from Damascus to the Euphrates.

† 'The gospel which was preached of me is not after man; for I neither received it of man, neither was I taught it, but by the revelation of Jesus Christ. —*Gal.* i. 11, 12.

THE ESCAPE IN A BASKET.

preach more boldly than ever about Jesus.

The Jews grew very angry at hearing him praise Jesus so much, and declare He was alive. They were so angry that they determined to try and kill him. But how could they do it?

They knew that the governor of Damascus was an enemy to Jesus. Aretas was the king of Arabia, and Damascus belonged to him. King Aretas lived far away from Damascus, but he had placed a governor in Damascus, with many soldiers under him.*

The Jews went to the governor and told him they wanted to kill Saul. They asked him to lend them soldiers to help them to seize Saul. They placed some soldiers at one of the gates, and some more soldiers at another of the gates, and they commanded them to

---

* 'In Damascus the governor under Aretas the king kept the city of the Damascenes with a garrison, desirous to apprehend me.'—2 *Cor*. xi. 32.

stay there night as well as day, and to seize Saul if he came near. Saul heard of these soldiers being at the gates, so he did not try to go through the gates.

The believers in Damascus loved Saul, and they found out a way of saving him from the unbelieving Jews.

They took him to a house built by the wall, with a window looking out of the city into the fields. To this house they took Saul secretly. There were large baskets in the city, used for holding rubbish before it was thrown away. Into such a large basket Saul got in, and he was then let down by a rope into the fields. It was in the night when he was let down.

Saul got out of the basket and walked about—a lonely traveller.

He set his face to go to Jerusalem. Whom did he wish to see there? Peter. He wanted to see Peter, who had preached the first sermon after Christ's resurrection.

THE ESCAPE IN A BASKET.

So he set out on his journey, walking over the same ground that he had gone over three years ago.

But how different he was three years ago from what he is now!

Then he was proud—now he is very humble; then he had all the priests for his friends—now he has them for his enemies; then he hated Jesus—now he loves Him more than his own life. How thankful he feels to God as he walks along the road to Jerusalem! Though alone, he is not unhappy—though poor, he feels rich—though many want to kill him, he is not afraid.

'Through a window in a basket was I let down by the wall, and escaped his hands.'—2 *Cor.* xi. 33.

Whose hands? The hands of the governor of Damascus under Aretas, king of Arabia.

XV.

SAUL'S VISIT TO PETER.

Acts, ix. 26, 27. Gal. i. 18, 19.

AFTER a journey of many days through the land of Israel, Saul arrived at Jerusalem. When he had last been there, what harm he had done in the city! But now he came to do good, and to save sinners by his preaching.

He wanted first to see Peter. But he did not know Peter. So he went to the disciples, or believers. There were so many of them that it was easy to find them. Some of them remembered his cruel conduct in old times when he lived there, and how he helped at the stoning of Stephen.

When Saul told them that he had been changed, the disciples did not believe him; they thought he was deceiving them by pretending to be a believer; they thought he wanted to find them out, and then to give them up to the high priest. How much Saul must have been grieved at the sheep taking him for a wolf, when he was now a sheep himself!

One of the disciples was of a very kind disposition, kinder than the rest (though all were kind). His name was Barnabas. He had pity on Saul, and he believed all he said. He said to Saul, 'Do you want to see Peter? I will bring you to him.' So Barnabas took him by the hand and led him to Peter's house. There was only one other apostle in Jerusalem—James (the brother of Jude), who wrote the Epistle. Barnabas brought Saul to Peter and James, and told them of the light that once shone near Damascus, and how Jesus was seen in the heaven, and how He said to Saul, 'Why persecutest thou me?' He related the whole of the wonderful history. Then Peter believed that Saul was sincere, and he asked Saul to stay at his house fifteen days. And James, too, was kind to Saul. It was pleasant to see the apostles giving their right hands to Saul and Barnabas, and receiving them as brothers. From this time they might all be seen going about Jerusalem together.

'Receive ye one another, as Christ also received us, to the glory of God.'—*Rom.* xv. 7.

XVI.

THE WARNING DREAM.

Acts, ix. 28–30; xxii. 17–21.

THERE could not be a happier season than was enjoyed by the four believing friends going about Jerusalem. Peter and James, Saul and Barnabas, were now most affectionate friends. Which would you have liked best to be with?

THE WARNING DREAM.

I must tell you a little more of Barnabas. His name had been Joses. It was changed to Barnabas, or rather Barnabas was added to Joses, so that his name was now Joses Barnabas. Why? Barnabas means 'Son of Consolation, or Comfort.' This was his character, as he showed in his behaviour towards Saul. He was a Jew, even a Levite. He had fields, and sold them, that the money might be given to the poor. He did not give it to the poor himself; he laid it down at the apostles' feet, that the apostles might give it to whom they chose. A man might do all this and yet have no charity or love in his heart; then his gifts would be worthless, for it is written, 'Though I bestow all my goods to feed the poor, and have not charity, it profiteth me nothing.' But Barnabas was full of love in his heart. How much Saul must have loved him for bringing him to Peter!

It was a great pleasure for Saul to get acquainted with Peter, for Peter knew the Lord well, while that Lord was a man of sorrows on earth, but Saul had only seen Him in glory. Of those four friends, two had known Him well on earth, and two had believed on Him after he was ascended; at least we suppose that Barnabas had only lately believed, and we know that Saul was an enemy until lately.

And where was the loving John? He was not in Jerusalem, so Saul had not the pleasure at this time of seeing him.

Saul could not spend all his time in talking with his dear friends about Jesus. He desired to preach to the unbelievers.

Saul preached boldly in Jerusalem, and he made the Jews very angry by declaring that Jesus was the Son of God. They began, like the Jews in Damascus, to make plans to kill him

THE WARNING DREAM. 77

secretly, but the Lord saved him from being murdered.

One day Saul was in the Temple praying, when the Lord sent him a dream, and said to him, 'Make haste, and go quickly out of Jerusalem, for the Jews will not believe what you say about me.' Saul was surprised, and he said, 'Do not they know how I once put believers in prison, and beat them; and how I was standing by when the blood of Thy martyr Stephen was shed, and how I kept the clothes of those who killed him?' But the Lord still said, 'Depart, for I will send you far away to the Gentiles.'

Then Saul told his friends that he must leave Jerusalem, for the Lord had commanded him to go away, because the Jews intended to kill him.

When the disciples heard this they were very anxious to send him away. They took him down secretly to the sea-side. There was a fine town built in honour of the Roman Emperor Cæsar, and it was called Cæsarea. Saul had to go about a hundred miles to this town. He must at first have travelled by night to hide himself from the Jews.

What good man was living there who would be glad to see Saul? Philip the deacon. Perhaps he had not seen Saul since the stoning of Stephen. How much changed Saul was since that time! That fierce, proud countenance, was now gentle, afflicted, and humble.

But perhaps Saul had no time to visit Philip at Cæsarea, for his friends were in great haste to send him far away. There were ships embarking from Cæsarea. One was setting sail for Tarsus. That was his native place, and there Saul wished now to go. How far was it off? Three hundred miles over the seas. Saul got into a ship. At last he came to land. He did not get out of the ship there; he had to sail twelve miles more up a river, till he came to a great mountain. Here was Tarsus. Here was his home. Here he had played when a child in his parents' sight. What would his old playfellows say when they heard he believed in Jesus?

'The Jews, who both killed the Lord Jesus and their own prophets, and have persecuted us.'—1 *Thess.* ii. 15.

XVII.

THE CHARITABLE WOMAN.

Acts, ix. 31 to end.

Now we must leave Saul at Tarsus, and return to Peter. We heard last of his being at Jerusalem when Saul paid his visit there. But Peter was not always there, for the apostles used to go on journeys to preach.

Once Peter went to a village among the hills, just twenty miles from Jerusalem. It was called Lydda. There were some of Christ's holy people living there, and Peter liked to visit them. One man was very ill indeed. His name was Æneas. He had the palsy, and he was so helpless that he had kept his bed eight years. Peter went to him, and said, 'Æneas, Jesus Christ maketh thee well. Arise, and make thy bed.' Immediately Æneas arose, and made his bed.

You observe that Peter did not say, '*I* make thee well;' for he knew he had no power in himself.

All the people round about wished to see Æneas; and when they saw this poor paralytic become quite strong they turned to the Lord.

But Peter did another great miracle. About twelve miles from Lydda there was a town by the sea-side, called Joppa. Some people from Lydda went

ACTS, IX. 34.

'And Peter said unto him, Æneas, Jesus Christ maketh thee whole; arise, and make thy bed.'

THE CHARITABLE WOMAN. 83

to Joppa, and said to the people there, 'The apostle Peter has come to see us, and he has cured a poor man who could not move a limb, and made him quite strong, by the power of Jesus.'

When the people of Joppa heard this—they wished much to see Peter, for a very good woman had just died at Joppa. Her name was Tabitha. She was so kind to poor people that many mourned her death. Her friends washed her dead body, and laid her in an upper room—the best room in the house. O how they longed to bring her to life! Some one said, 'O if Peter would but come! O let us send to beg him to come!'

So the disciples in Joppa sent two men to beg Peter to come very quickly before Tabitha was buried.

Peter came immediately with the two men. He was led into the upper chamber. He heard much weeping and sobbing as he was coming in, and he found the room full of poor widows and saints, the holy friends of Tabitha. The widows showed Peter a great many clothes that they held in their hands, and told him that Tabitha had woven the clothes while she was with them. The name they gave her was Dorcas. They loved Dorcas very much for spending her time in weaving for them.

Peter would not let the widows, or the saints, remain in the room. He wanted to pray to God alone. So he put the widows and saints out of the room, and when he was quiet and alone he kneeled down and prayed to God, and then he went up to Tabitha's bed, and said, 'Tabitha, arise!' She opened her eyes, and she saw Peter. Then she sat up. Peter gave her his hand to help her up.

As soon as she was standing up he called the widows in, as well as the saints, and showed them their friend.

ACTS, ix. 39.

'And all the widows stood by him weeping, and showing the coats and garments which Dorcas made while she was with them.'

What must have been the delight of all to see her alive! No doubt Dorcas made many more clothes for poor widows before she died again. It was sad for her to die twice, but then her being made alive caused many sinners to turn to the Lord.

Peter did not return to Jerusalem for a long time afterwards, but he took a lodging in Joppa. It was by the sea-side, at the house of a man called Simon. This Simon was a tanner. His trade was to make skins into leather.

Tabitha must have been glad that Peter stayed in Joppa to teach her more about Jesus and His salvation.

'Who can find a virtuous woman? for her price is far above rubies. . . . She stretcheth out her hand to the poor; yea, she reacheth forth her hands to the needy.'—*Prov.* xxxi. 10, 20.

XVIII.

THE VISION ON THE HOUSETOP.

Acts, x. 8-23.

WHILE Peter was living at Joppa he lodged, you know, with Simon the tanner. He went up one day to the top of the house, which was flat. He wanted to be alone. There was often a little tent in the corner of the housetop, where a man could be shaded from the sun and hidden from all.

Peter went up about twelve o'clock to pray to God. He had taken no breakfast that morning, for he wished to fast as well as to pray. After some time he became very hungry, so he asked the servants to get his dinner ready immediately. While they were getting it ready, he fell into a sort of sleep upon the housetop.

He had a very strange dream in his sleep. He thought that the sky was opened, and that there was let down out of it a great sheet, with the four corners fastened, so that the sheet could hold things. Inside there were all kinds of four-footed beasts, and some of them were wild; and all kinds of birds, and all kinds of creeping things. What a strange heap they must all have looked in the sheet!

Then Peter heard a voice, saying, 'Rise, Peter; kill and eat.' Peter was surprised at hearing this command, for God had given the Jews very strict rules about eating. He had forbidden them to eat of beasts called unclean, such as pigs, hares, horses, and asses. Among birds He had forbidden the Jews to eat of eagles, owls, swans, storks, and many others; and also He had forbidden them to eat of creeping things, lizards, snails, and moles.

So when Peter had looked well at these unclean animals, he answered the voice, 'Not so, Lord; for I have never eaten anything that is common or unclean.' The voice from heaven replied, 'Whatever God has made clean, call not thou common.'

Three times the voice spoke these words, and then the great sheet of animals was taken up again into heaven.

When the dream was over, Peter went on thinking about it, and wondering what could be the meaning of it.

At the time the Spirit spoke to his mind, saying: 'Three men are come to thy house, and they want you to go with them. Go with them, for I have sent them.'

Then Peter went down the stairs from the housetop, and he found three men waiting to see him, just as the Spirit had told him.

He said to them, 'I am the person you want to see. Why are you come for me?'

THE VISION ON THE HOUSETOP.

Then the three men replied :—

'Cornelius, a very good man, was told by a holy angel to send for you to come to his house, that you might tell him how he may be saved.'*

Peter found that these men were the servants of Cornelius, and that Cornelius was a great captain. The three men were not Jews; and Cornelius, the master, was not a Jew. They were all Romans. Now the Jews called all nations—Gentiles; and they despised them all as common or unclean. Peter saw why the dream had been sent to him; he saw that God did not call these men common or unclean. So Peter promised to go with them.

'My name shall be great among the Gentiles.'—*Mal.* i. 11.

* See Acts, xi. 14.

XIX.

PETER'S VISIT TO CORNELIUS.

Acts, x. 23 to end.

The three men told Peter they came from Cæsarea, a town fifty miles off. They had not been able to walk so far in one day; so they had slept on the way.

Peter asked them to stop that night, and to sleep in the house where he lodged, and he promised to go with them next day.

He went and told his friends in Joppa what had happened. He said to them, 'I wish you would go with me to Cæsarea to see Cornelius, the Roman captain.'

Six of them consented to go with him. Next day the whole party set out on their journey. There were Peter and the six Jews, his friends; there were also the three servants of Cornelius — they were Gentiles. How many were there in all? Ten. What did they talk of on the way? It must have been of Jesus. How much Peter had to tell about Him, as he had lived with Him!

The travellers walked about twenty miles along the sea-coast, and then they rested for the night, though we know not where. Next day they set out again; and they arrived at Cæsarea in the afternoon.

Cæsarea was a very grand town among the rocks of the sea-shore. It was Herod who had made it so grand, and he had built a palace there. Peter did not go to that palace; he went straight up to the house of Cornelius.

It was four days since Cornelius had seen the angel in his house.

Cornelius knew that his servants would be two days going to Joppa, and two days in coming back. So he was expecting Peter to arrive that afternoon; and he had invited all his relatives and his dearest friends to come to his house that day.

When he heard that Peter was at the gate, he went out to meet him. When he saw him, he did not shake hands (as we do with our friends); nor did he embrace him, but he fell at his feet and worshipped him. Peter did not approve this. He give him his hand, saying, 'Stand up; for I myself also am a man.'

Then Cornelius led him into a large room, filled with his friends and relations. They were all Gentiles.

Once Peter would not have gone into a room with one Gentile; but now he would go to Gentiles, just the same as to Jews. He told these Gentiles of his dream, and how the angel had said, 'What God hath cleansed, that call not thou common.'

Then Peter asked Cornelius to tell him why he had sent for him.

Cornelius spoke to Peter before all the company, saying, 'Four days ago I had taken no food, and at three o'clock I prayed in my house, and behold a man stood before me in bright clothing, and he said, " Cornelius, thy prayer is heard, and thy charity to the poor is remembered by God. Send to Joppa, and ask for a man named Simon Peter. He lodges in the house of Simon a tanner, by the sea-side. Ask him to come here. When he comes he will tell thee what thou must do." So I sent immediately for thee; and thou hast done right in coming. We are all assembled here to listen to all that God has commanded thee to say to us.'

Then Peter began to preach to these Gentiles. He told them about Jesus; how the Jews had killed Him, and how God had raised Him from the dead.

Peter ended his sermon with these words : 'Whosoever believeth in Him shall receive forgiveness of sins.'

As soon as Peter had spoken, the Holy Ghost fell on all the Gentiles in the room, just as once He had fallen on the Jews; and these Gentiles began to praise God in many strange languages.

The six Jews who had come with Peter were very much astonished at seeing that God gave the Holy Ghost to Gentiles.

Then Peter said, 'Can any man forbid us to baptize these men with water, now they have received the Holy Ghost as we did?' So he had them baptized. No doubt it was the six Jews from Joppa who baptized them.

Ever since that time, Gentiles have always been baptized when they believed in Jesus.

We are Gentiles; (for most of those who read this book are not Jews.) What a great mercy it is for us that God has made no difference between Jews and Gentiles! but loved them all the same — if they believe in Him.

'Salvation is come unto the Gentiles.'—*Rom.* xi. 11.

XX.

PETER'S DELIVERANCE.

Acts, xii. 1-17.

PETER stayed a good while with Cornelius and his friends at Cæsarea. He had a great deal to teach them, and they were anxious to learn. After a while he went again to Jerusalem. He told the saints in Jerusalem all about Cornelius, and those good men were very much pleased, and praised God, saying, 'God hath given repentance unto the Gentiles!'

But very great troubles soon came upon the saints in Jerusalem. Cæsar at Rome appointed Herod to be king of Jerusalem and of all the land.

Who was this Herod?

He was not the Herod who killed John the Baptist, and mocked Jesus the Saviour. That Herod had been sent far away by the Emperor Cæsar. This Herod was his nephew, and he was the grandson of the Herod who killed, long ago, the babes of Bethlehem. What a wicked family these Herods were! This Herod commanded his soldiers to seize James, the brother of John, and to cut off his head with a sword.

So now John lost his brother. Those two brothers had been with Jesus on the mount of glory and in the garden of agony. James was one of the three favourites of the Lord, though John was the most beloved of all. He was the first of all the apostles to be killed for the sake of Jesus.

Herod saw that the Jews were pleased

with him for killing James, so he thought he would kill Peter too; and he sent soldiers to seize him and to put him in prison: but, as he had heard of his once escaping from prison, he desired sixteen soldiers to guard him night and day.

Herod fixed the day when Peter was to be killed. The night before that terrible day the saints met together to pray for him. The other apostles had left Jerusalem, lest they also should be killed; but there were many saints still there. They met together in the house of a very good woman, named Mary. She was not one of the Marys we have heard of before. She was the sister of that good Barnabas who had once been so kind to Saul.

Mary and her friends were sitting up all the night. Peter was quietly sleeping in prison. It was the beginning of summer, and it was warm. Peter had taken off his sandals and his upper garment, but he could not take off a chain from each hand, which was fastened to a soldier's hand on each side of him. Suddenly an angel made the dark prison brighter than the day. Yet Peter was so sound asleep, that he did not wake, till the angel touched him, saying, 'Arise up quickly.' And as Peter rose up—the chains fell off his hands.

Then the angel bade him tighten his clothes round his waist, put on his sandals, and wrap himself in his loose upper garment. All this time the soldiers slept.

The angel said, 'Follow me.' Peter followed, feeling as if he were dreaming. The angel led him past many soldiers that had been placed to watch outside, and brought him to the great iron gate. Though it had bolts and bars it opened without key and without hand—as if it had opened itself.

Acts, xii. 13.

'A damsel came to hearken, named Rhoda.'

The angel brought him down one street and then departed.

When Peter found himself alone he stopped to think of what had happened. He saw that God had set him free, and saved him from death. He had heard that the saints were sitting up at night to pray for him in Mary's house. So he went there. He knocked at the door of the porch, and Rhoda the maid came to the door. You know the history—how, when she heard Peter's voice outside, saying, 'Let me in,' her joy was so great that she forgot to open the door, but ran into the house to tell his friends that Peter was there—and how they would not believe her, but said it was some angel that took care of Peter.

Peter, however, went on knocking, till many friends rushed to the door and saw his face. They were inclined to make much noise in their joy, but Peter made a sign for them to be quiet, as noise might have been heard by their enemies. When they were quiet, Peter told them how the Lord had delivered him. He then said, 'Go and tell this to James and the brethren.'

It was James the brother of Jude that he meant,—the same James that Saul had seen. Then Peter went away to some place that Herod did not know of.

God still hears the prayers of His people, and delivers them in different ways out of the hands of their enemies.

'The eyes of the Lord are over the righteous, and his ears are open unto their prayers.'—1 *Pet.* iii. 12.

XXI.

THE DEATH OF THE THIRD HEROD.
Acts, xii. 18-23.

As soon as it was day the soldiers were ready to lead Peter out to die, but they could not find him. They could not think what had become of him.

Herod heard that Peter was missing, just as he was expecting to see him led forth in chains. He sent for the soldiers who had the charge of him, and asked them where he was; and when they could not tell him, he had them all put to death instead of Peter.

Afterwards this cruel man made a journey to Cæsarea. That was the place where Cornelius lived. It was a very grand city, and there was a grand palace in it for King Herod.

There was another grand building in it, where the multitude often came to see shows of men wrestling, and beasts fighting.

Herod's chief servant was named Blastus. This Blastus told Herod that some men were come from Tyre in a ship, and that these men wanted to ask the king's pardon for something they had done to affront him.

Herod agreed to see the men from Tyre, and he fixed a day for their coming to the grand building. A multitude assembled to hear Herod speak to the men of Tyre. There were stone seats for the multitude from the floor to the ceiling, all round this vast hall, and there was a great purple throne for Herod in the midst.

Herod wished to look very splendid and glorious that day. He was dressed in glittering robes of silver, which when the sun shone dazzled the eyes of the beholders.* Blastus brought in the men of Tyre to hear the king's speech.

* Josephus.

DEATH OF THE THIRD HEROD.

Then Herod made a speech to the people, and he used such fine words that the people shouted, and cried out, 'It is the voice of a god and not of a man!' This was a wicked thing to say. I am sure if Cornelius was there he did not join in the shout. Herod felt pleased with the words. He liked to be thought a god.

But God was so much displeased with the words that He sent His angel to make Herod ill that very moment. He felt such horrible pain that he could not stay on his throne, and he was carried by his servants to his bed. Then his flesh was eaten by worms while he was still alive. No doctor could cure him, and in five days he died. Thus every one saw how unlike he was to a god.

God showed by sending him this loathsome disease how much He hates pride—even a proud thought. His sin was—liking to be called a god, and not giving Jesus the glory. Was it not a proud thought to like to be called a god?

We have heard of three Herods, and all were very wicked.

The first killed the babes of Bethlehem.

The second killed John the Baptist.

And the third killed James and mocked Jesus, and would have killed Peter if he could.

They were all proud of being kings, and they all hated the true King of the Jews.

'Because thine heart is lifted up, and thou hast said, "I am a god;" yet thou art a man and not a god.'—*Ezek*. xxviii. 2.

XXII.

THE CHRISTIANS OF ANTIOCH.

Acts, xi. 19 to end.

Do you remember where Saul had gone when he left Jerusalem? He had gone to his own country—his native country—Tarsus.

At Tarsus he had played when he was a little boy—at Tarsus he had sat on his mother's knee—at Tarsus he had been taught to repeat his first Jewish prayers.

Now he could tell his parents (if they were alive) about Jesus; now he could tell his old playmates about Him who was crucified at Jerusalem a little while ago. But he knew he must not stay there always, for God had chosen him to preach to all nations.

One day a man arrived in Tarsus, inquiring for Saul. Who was this man? Saul's kindest friend. When the apostles had turned away from Saul this man had taken him by the hand, and begged them to receive him as a brother. This man was Barnabas. His name was 'Son of Consolation, or Comfort.' Was not Saul glad to see him? O yes!—glad indeed.

Barnabas had a great deal to tell him. He told him that he had come from a heathen city, where many people had turned unto the Lord. 'Come with me,' said he, 'to the city of Antioch; for we want you there to teach the heathen who have just turned to the Lord.'

Saul willingly went with Barnabas to the city of Antioch, in Syria. It was a very grand city, full of fine houses, and beautiful gardens, and heathen temples; but there were quiet rooms in it, where many believers met together to worship the Father and the Son.

In this city a new name was given to

believers in Christ. They were called Christians, and they have kept that name, even to this day.

Saul and Barnabas spent a whole year in Antioch, preaching to the new Christians. Once only they took a journey to Jerusalem. The Christians at Antioch sent them there to give money to poor saints, as bread was very scarce and dear. This was a proof of their love for Jesus, as it was at Jerusalem that Jesus died and rose again.

'And the disciples were called Christians first at Antioch.'— *Acts*, xi. end of 26.

XXIII.

PAUL'S FIRST MISSIONARY JOURNEY.

Acts, xiii. 1–12.

WHILE Saul and Barnabas were living at Antioch, in Syria, the Holy Ghost said to the Christian teachers, 'Let Barnabas and Saul go to the work I have called them to do.' So the other Christian teachers prayed, and sent them out to preach to the heathen.

And they took with them a young man, named John Mark. He was the nephew of Barnabas, and his uncle was fond of him, and liked to have him with him.

Where did they first go?

They went to the native country of Barnabas. Saul had once gone to his native country, Tarsus, and now Barnabas wished to go to his. Barnabas had been born in a very large and beautiful island, called Cyprus.

Saul and Barnabas sailed to Cyprus in a ship. They could easily get there in a day. When they landed at Salamis, the port, they found themselves among orange-groves and apricot-gardens. The hills were covered with vines, and the green pastures were sprinkled over with milk-white flocks. But this sweet country was made hateful by the wicked ways of its people. The two apostles preached everywhere they could. They went all through the island preaching. The island is about one hundred miles long.

At the further end, there was a city called Paphos, where the governor lived. His name was Sergius Paulus. He was a Roman, and was king or governor under Cæsar at Rome—just as Pontius Pilate had been king in Jerusalem.

But he was a much wiser man than Pilate. When he heard of the preaching of the wonderful strangers, he wanted to hear them preach, and so he sent for them, that he might learn about the true God.

The two apostles went into the palace of the governor, hoping to lead him to believe in Jesus.

There was a very wicked man in

the room. His name was Bar-jesus. He was a Jew, and had a Jewish name, meaning the 'Son of Jesus,' but he was really the son of Satan. He had another name, meaning 'Wise Man'— Elymas—for he pretended that he was wise through the devil, and he pretended to do wonders. He was a wizard, or one who knew the wise art. He was a sorcerer and a conjurer. This wicked Jew could not bear to hear of Jesus, and he tried to turn away the governor from believing in him. We do not know what he said, only that he spoke against the Gospel.

Saul then turned towards him, and fixed his eyes upon him, saying, 'O full of all cunning and mischief, thou child of the devil, thou enemy of all righteousness! the hand of the Lord is upon thee, and thou shalt be blind and not see the sun for a season.'

Immediately this wicked man found himself in darkness, and he spread out

Acts, xiii. 11.

'And immediately there fell on him a mist and a darkness; and he went about seeking some one to lead him by the hand.'

his hands, looking for some one to lead him by the hand.

The governor, when he saw this miracle, believed in the Lord.

What a just punishment this sorcerer had! He tried to keep the governor in darkness of heart that he should not see the Light of the world.

How this punishment must have reminded Saul of the time when he was made blind!

Saul hoped that this sorcerer might have his sight restored one day, for he said to him, 'Thou shalt not see the sun for *a season.*' He did not say he should never see it again; but no one knows whether Bar-jesus ever repented, or whether he died a blind sinner.

'The god of this world hath blinded the minds of them which believe not.'—2 *Cor.* iv. 4.

XXIV.

THE UNFAITHFUL COMPANION.

Acts, xiii. 13–16, 38–50.

After this visit to Cyprus you will never hear Saul spoken of any more. From this time his name is Paul. No one knows why his name was changed; perhaps it was because Paul was a Roman name, and suited him, now he preached to the Romans and other Gentiles. Saul was only a Jewish name.

Paul and Barnabas soon left the island of Cyprus. They wanted to go from land to land to preach the Gospel. They set sail from Paphos, crossed the sea in a ship, and came to the great country called Asia. They landed near a town called Perga, on the banks of a river, under high and steep rocks.

Beyond — they saw great mountains with tops covered with snow.

It was at Perga that John Mark gave great sorrow to his uncle and to Paul. He said he would go back to Jerusalem, where his mother Mary lived.

What was his reason? He was not ill. *Then*—he would have had a good reason for going away.

It is most likely he was afraid to go on. Perhaps he did not like the thought of climbing up those snowy mountains, nor creeping along dark rocky paths, where robbers lay hid in the caves, ready to burst out upon travellers. Perhaps he was afraid lest other men as wicked as Bar-jesus should scoff at him, and put him in prison or kill him. We cannot tell what were the feelings of John Mark, but of this we are sure, he had not courage to bear the troubles of the way.

He found a ship going from Perga to the coast near Jerusalem, and he sailed in it. Did not his heart reproach him for leaving the holy apostles in the midst of their journey? We know not how *soon* he felt sorry for what he had done; but we know that in the end he became a brave and zealous man, and wrote the Gospel called by his name, Mark. This John Mark has the honour of being one of the four Evangelists.

Paul and Barnabas went on their journey together. They travelled on foot over cold mountains to a country called Pisidia.

They had left the mountains behind, and they had reached a wilderness scattered over with lakes and bogs. At last they came to a large city upon the top of a low hill. This city was called Antioch.

That is a name we have heard before. You have heard of Antioch in Syria; but this city was Antioch in Pisidia. The other Antioch was by the sea; this Antioch was on a flat land near the mountains.

On the Sabbath day the apostles go to the synagogue. It is a strange building of a round shape, with seats rising one above another. In the middle is a high wooden table, where an old man with a long beard reads out of a scroll he holds in his hand; he reads in Hebrew, and an interpreter translates into Greek; for all the people around understand Greek. After the old man, or the president, has done reading the scroll, he has it carefully rolled up and put into a large chest; he then sends a message to Paul and Barnabas, asking them to preach.

Paul rose up and began his sermon. He told the history of the Saviour's death and the resurrection. He said near the end of the sermon these words: 'Through this man is preached unto you the forgiveness of sins.'

The Jews were very angry at the sermon, and went out murmuring against Paul; but the Gentiles stayed behind to beg him to preach the next Sabbath about Jesus.

These Gentiles were called proselytes; they had already turned from idols to believe in the true God, and now they would not leave the apostles, but followed them about, hoping to hear more about Jesus.

Paul and Barnabas during the whole week tried to persuade those who believed to continue firm and steadfast in the faith of Jesus.

The second Sabbath of Paul's visit there was a great stir in the place; almost the whole city came to the synagogue to hear the word of God.

The Jews were so angry to see such a large congregation that they spoke against Jesus, and contradicted all that Paul said.

This wicked conduct displeased the two holy apostles. Before they left the synagogue they said, ' As the

Jews will not hear the word of God, we turn to the Gentiles.'

The Gentiles were glad to hear this, and many more believed. But the Jews grew more and more angry, till at last they made the preachers leave the city.

It will be terrible for those Jews at the Day of Judgment, for they ill-treated the messengers of God.

'Seeing it is a righteous thing with God to recompense tribulation to them that trouble you.' —2 *Thess.* i. 6.

XXV.

THE STONING.

Acts, xiii. 51, 52 ; xiv. 1-20.

WHEN the two apostles left Antioch in Pisidia they went to another city.

God gave the name of apostles to both of them; for though they were not of the number of the twelve they were both sent forth by the Holy Ghost, who is God (Acts, xiii. 2). None are called apostles but those whom God Himself—Father, Son, or Spirit—sent forth.

The apostles went on their way till they came to a city sixty miles off. It was called Iconium. The two apostles went again into a synagogue, and preached again to the Jews, and also to those Gentiles who had turned to the true God—the proselytes. But the unbelieving Jews set the Gentiles against the apostles and all the Christians.

The apostles stayed a long while in Iconium, and preached very boldly about Jesus, and did many miracles to prove that their word was true. There was so much strife between the unbelievers and the believers that it was very hard for the apostles to

Acts, xiv. 9, 10.

'The same heard Paul speak: who steadfastly beholding him, and perceiving that he had faith to be healed, said with a loud voice, Stand upright on thy feet.'

bear the treatment they met with; but they were ready to suffer anything, if they might but save some souls.

At last they knew that a plan was made by their enemies to stone them. Then they thought it was right for them to escape. They left Iconium and passed through a country where shepherds fed their flocks, till they came to a town named Lystra. The people of Lystra had taken Jupiter for their god, and had built him a handsome temple, and had placed in it an ivory image of Jupiter—as a very fine, grand-looking man.

In Lystra the apostles preached the gospel. A poor cripple, who had never walked, sat at Paul's feet while he was preaching. He believed in Jesus crucified for his sins. Paul fixed his eyes on him, and seeing he had faith, he said with a loud voice, 'Stand upright on thy feet!' Immediately the man sprang up and began to walk.

When the people saw what Paul had done they cried out, 'The gods have come down to us, looking like men!' This was said in the common language of the people of the country, and not in Greek. The apostles did not understand what the people said, or *they* would have told them at once that they were not gods.

So the apostles went to their home in the city, while the people went to the idol priest, to ask him to bring oxen and garlands of flowers to the gates. When Paul and Barnabas heard that oxen were going to be sacrificed to them they were very much grieved.

The people thought Barnabas was Jupiter, the King of Heaven, because he was tall and grand-looking; and they thought Paul was Mercury, because he spoke well — and Mercury was the god of fine speaking.

The apostles were dreadfully hurt when they knew that the oxen were to be sacrificed in their honour, and they tore their clothes, and ran in among the people, saying, 'We are men like yourselves, and we preach that you may turn to the true God who made heaven and earth.' Yet the apostles could hardly persuade the people to give up their plan of sacrificing to them.

But they had not long to suffer from being too much honoured, for those who would have been their worshippers were easily changed into their murderers.

And this is how it came to pass.

Some Jews came from Antioch, and some Jews came from Iconium, full of hatred against the apostles. They easily set the people of Lystra against them. Nothing now would satisfy these wicked men but killing the apostles. They stoned Paul upon the spot. When he seemed dead they dragged his body out of the city. The believers would not leave that dear body, but stood over it lamenting—suddenly the body moved—rose up, and walked into the city. What joy for Barnabas and all who loved Paul!

He stayed one night only among his murderers. The next day he left for Lystra, accompanied by Barnabas. Paul must have felt great pain while he was being stoned. Did he not then think of Stephen, whose pain he once witnessed? *Then* he rejoiced at the sight,—*now* he bitterly lamented the sin.

'Once was I stoned.'—2 *Cor.* xi. 25.

XXVI.

PAUL'S SHORT JOURNEY TO JERUSALEM.

Acts, xiv. 20 to end; xv. 1-6, 31.

WHAT a terrible event was the stoning at Lystra!

ACTS, xiv. 20.
'Howbeit, as the disciples stood round about him, he rose up, and came into the city.'

Did Paul go on his journey after that? Yes, he did. He went to one city more, called Derbe. There the apostles preached the gospel and taught many.

Then they determined to return by the way they came. They saw again the believers in Lystra, in Iconium, and in Antioch in Pisidia.

Everywhere Paul and Barnabas entreated the believers to continue trusting in Jesus. They appointed elders to teach, and they prayed with them, and commended them to the Lord. At last they came to Perga, where John Mark had once left them. From a port near Perga they set sail, and came back to Antioch in Syria.

When they were returned they asked all the Christians to come together to hear them give an account of their journey. They told the Christians about Sergius Paulus, in the island of Cyprus, and of many more Gentiles turning to the Lord.

Paul and Barnabas lived in Antioch in Syria for a long while, teaching the word of the Lord. During the time they lived at Antioch they once paid a visit to Jerusalem. The reason they went there was to settle a dispute. This was the dispute:—

Some Jews came down to Antioch, saying that Gentiles ought to observe all the ceremonies that Moses taught, such as sacrifices and circumcision. Paul and Barnabas said that Gentiles need not observe these laws of Moses. But the other Jews would not agree to what they said. So Paul and Barnabas, and some other holy men, went to Jerusalem to consult the apostles. As they went along they preached at places by the way, and told the history of the conversion of many Gentiles. What they related caused great joy among the brethren.

When Paul and Barnabas arrived at Jerusalem they saw many believers, and told them the same history. Paul had seen Peter and James before, but now he saw John for the first time.

What joy for Paul to see him who had leaned on Jesus' bosom!

All the apostles and elders agreed to meet together to consider about the Gentiles keeping the old laws of Moses. All the apostles were of one mind about not troubling the Gentiles with the ceremonies of Moses. The apostles wrote a letter to the brethren in Antioch, saying what they thought. Paul and Barnabas and other brethren took this letter back to Antioch, and they read it at a meeting of the brethren. All who heard this letter were much comforted.

'Do all things without murmurings and disputings.'—*Phil.* ii. 14.

XXVII.

PAUL'S SECOND MISSIONARY JOURNEY.

Acts, xv. 36 to end ; xvi. 1–3.

WHEN Paul and Barnabas were leaving Jerusalem they took with them several holy men. One of these was a prophet, called Silas. He became a great friend of Paul's, and he liked to stay with him at Antioch when the other brethren went back to Jerusalem.

At last Paul said to Barnabas, 'Let us go again and see the people to whom we preached in our journey.' Barnabas was quite ready to go. The next question was, 'Who shall go with us?' Barnabas said, 'I will take my nephew, John Mark.' 'No,' said Paul, 'he shall not go with us.' 'Why not?' said Barnabas. 'Because he left us on our journey.' Barnabas said that he would like to try him again. But Paul would not try him again.

ACTS, xv. 39.

'And the contention was so sharp between them, that they departed asunder one from the other.'

Neither Paul nor Barnabas would give up to the other. At the end it was settled that they must part from one another. Barnabas took Mark with him and set sail for Cyprus, his own country, where he had once preached the gospel.

Paul chose for his companion Silas, the prophet, and he went to his own country, Tarsus, where he had once preached the gospel.

He went over some very high mountains, called Taurus (or the bull)—mountains with caps of snow on their heads, and he soon came to Lystra, where he had once been stoned. He was not afraid of going there again. This was his third visit. This time the people neither stoned him, nor wanted to offer sacrifice to him.

Here he found a young man named Timothy. He felt a great affection for this Timothy. Timothy's mother was a Jewess. She had taught Timothy to know the Scriptures when he was quite a child. His grandmother also had taught him. But he did not know about Jesus till Paul preached at Lystra the first time, just before he was stoned. Paul heard a very good character of Timothy from all the Christians at Lystra. He wished very much to have him as a companion on his journey. Timothy was quite ready to go. These two were like father and son. Paul had no son of his own, and he was glad to have Timothy for his son. He called him his dearly beloved son.

Now there were three travelling together—Paul, Silas, and young Timothy. On the first journey there were three also, Paul, Barnabas, and young Mark. But Timothy was more faithful than Mark had been. He was indeed a comfort to Paul.

Paul long afterwards reminded Timothy, 'Of persecutions, afflictions, which came unto me at Antioch, at Iconium, at Lystra; what persecutions I endured: but out of them all the Lord delivered me.'—2 *Tim.* iii. 11.

XXVIII.

THE WOMAN FULL OF PRAYERS.

Acts, xvi. 8-15.

THESE three friends travelled all about Asia together. I do not mean the great Asia, but the little Asia that you will see in the map just above Cyprus.

One day they came to a town called Troas. It was by the sea-coast.

One night Paul had a wonderful dream. He saw a man standing and speaking very earnestly to him, saying, 'Come over and help us.' He knew that the man came from Macedonia. Perhaps the man in the dream said where he came from, or perhaps Paul knew by his dress and language to what country he belonged. When Paul awoke he told his dream to his companions. How many companions had he? Two—Silas and Timothy. Now he had a fourth, named Luke.

We do not know where he first saw Luke. Paul must have been very glad to get Luke for a companion. Luke was a very learned, clever man, and he wrote this history we are reading from the Bible; yes—it was Luke who wrote the Acts. He wrote also one of the histories of our Saviour, and for that reason he is called the 'Evangelist'— for the four men who wrote the four histories of Jesus are called the 'Evangelists.' Luke was a physician and doctor. Paul called him the 'beloved Physician.'

There were now *four* travellers. I need not repeat their names. They must have been happy together, praying and singing hymns to Jesus. The four friends set sail in a little ship. They were two days on the voyage. The second day they arrived at the sea-coast of Macedonia, the country of the man in the dream.

They went to a fine city called Philippi. It was built on a great plain close by a river. Very few Jews lived in this city, so there was no synagogue in it. But there was a little house for prayer close by the river-side.

On the Sabbath-day—which was Saturday—the four ministers went to this prayer-house. They found a few women at the prayer-meeting. The men, perhaps, would not come.

The ministers sat down and spoke to the women. There was one woman there who listened most attentively. Her name was Lydia. Her trade was selling a purple dye fit for the robes of kings. This woman came from Asia to sell her purple dye, but she discovered in that meeting a treasure more precious than the purple of kings. She found the Lord Jesus. While Paul was speaking about His love, God opened Lydia's heart.

After the service she spoke to Paul, and told him that she believed in Jesus, and that she wished to be baptized. Paul approved of her so well that he had her baptized; and also her family and servants. Probably they were baptized in the river close by.

Then Lydia asked the four ministers to do her a great favour. It was, to come to her house and live there as long as they stayed in Philippi.

Was not this kind?

It would cost a great deal to get food for four men, but Lydia loved them all for the sake of Jesus. At first they refused; but she pressed them so much that they consented to come to her house.

Paul once said to the people of Philippi, 'I have you in my haert.'—*Philip.* i. 7.

ACTS, XVI. 15.

'If ye have judged me to be faithful to the Lord, come into my house, and abide there.'

XXIX.

THE STRIPES.

Acts, xvi. 16–24.

How happy were Paul and his friends when they first came to Philippi! You do not forget their names—Silas, Timothy, and Luke. Nobody ill-treated them, and Lydia loaded them with kindness. But soon there was a great change.

The four ministers went very often to the house of prayer. There they used to preach as well as pray.

A young slave-girl once met them as they were going, and she followed them, crying out, 'These men are the servants of God, who show unto us the way of salvation.'

How strange it was for a girl to cry out in this way in the streets! She was a poor, miserable girl. The devil had come into her, and made her say wonderful things. Her masters were wicked men, who sent her out to get money by saying what the devil told her. She was called a sorceress.

The four ministers were grieved to hear her words, but they said nothing at first.

Another day the young girl met the ministers again. Another day she met them again; and so she went on, following them, and calling after them, day after day.

One day Paul knew that Jesus would give him the power to cast out the spirit in the girl, so he turned and said, 'I command thee in the name of Jesus Christ to come out of her.' And immediately the spirit came out of her.

Was it not a happy thing for this poor girl to be delivered from the tormenting devil? Indeed it was. For though what she had said of Paul was true, she told many lies, by which she had got money for her masters.

ACTS, XVI. 18.
'But Paul, being grieved, turned and said to the spirit, I command thee, in the name of Jesus Christ, to come out of her.'

THE STRIPES. 151

Those wicked men grew very angry. They said, 'We shall get no more money by our slave telling people what will happen.' So they went to meet the good men. They caught hold of Paul and Silas, and dragged them to the market-place. They complained of them to the judges, saying, 'These men are Jews, and they are a great trouble to our city, for they teach us new customs.'

The multitude joined in abusing them. No doubt they did not like the girl being stopped from telling them what was going to happen, so they were very angry with Paul and Silas.

The judges were ready to please the people, and so, instead of judging them, they desired their men to *beat* them. The clothes of Paul and Silas were torn off their backs, and they were beaten with rods. Every stroke of the rod left a red stripe upon the flesh of these holy men. I do not know what number of stripes they had to bear, but the number was more than forty. It was only the Jews who gave no more than forty. The Gentiles gave any number of stripes.

The cruel judges sent Paul and Silas to prison with their stripes all bleeding, and they desired the keeper of the prison not to let them escape.

The keeper, or jailer, was as cruel as the judges. He gave them no food, nor did he bind up their wounds; but he thrust them into a dungeon underground, and placed their feet in the stocks. There they sat—unable to move their legs or to draw their feet out of the holes in the board—unable to lie down or to stand up.

Where were Luke and Timothy? They had not been seized by their enemies. How much grieved they must have been when they heard what had happened to their dear friends!

What must Timothy have felt for his father in the Lord!

'We were shamefully entreated* at Philippi.'—1 *Thess.* ii. 2.

XXX.

THE EARTHQUAKE.

Acts, xvi. 25-34.

PAUL and Silas were sitting in the stocks at night, when a sound was heard from their dungeon. Was it the voice of weeping and wailing? No, it was the voice of singing! And what was the singing about? It was the praises of God the prisoners were singing.

What could they praise God for? Did they praise Him for letting them

* Treated.

be thrust into a horrible dungeon? Yes! they praised Him for letting them suffer for the sake of Jesus, because they knew they should rejoice with Him when He came again in His glory.

The other prisoners heard them sing. They were most of them thieves or murderers—wicked men, who deserved to be punished. But now we hope the singing turned their hearts to God; for the apostles sang about Jesus. They sang such a song as, 'Worthy is the Lamb, for He was slain for us.'

Suddenly a dreadful sound was heard,—it was the earth moving up and down—it was an earthquake.

So great was the earthquake that it shook the dungeon, opened the doors, and undid the chains. The apostles found their feet were set free from the holes in the boards. They could easily run away. But they did not move, because they knew it was God's will

ACTS. XVI. 29.

'Then he called for a light, and sprang in.'

they should stay. Nor did any of the prisoners escape, though they easily could.

The keeper was asleep, and was awakened by the earthquake. When he saw the doors standing open he felt sure the prisoners must be gone. He knew he had been wrong in sleeping, and he felt afraid that he should be condemned to die by the rulers. So he took out his sword, and was just going to stab himself, when he heard a loud voice from the dungeon calling out, 'Do thyself no harm, for we are all here.' Great was his surprise. He called for a light, and sprang into the dungeon, and fell down trembling at the feet of Paul and Silas—those feet he had once cruelly thrust into the stocks.

Immediately he brought them out of the dungeon, and said to them, 'Sirs, what must I do to be saved?' He wanted now to save his soul. Paul and Silas answered, 'Believe in the Lord Jesus Christ and thou shalt be saved, and all thy family and servants.'

The jailer had heard before that Jesus died to save him, and now he wished to be baptized. But first he washed the prisoners' stripes, and then was baptized with all his family. This must have been done with some water in the court of the prison.

Afterwards the jailer took the prisoners into his own house, and he brought them food. While they were sitting at supper he felt great joy at the thought of his Saviour, and so did all his family. That was a happy supper-table, for all who sat around it loved Jesus.

'Rejoice, inasmuch as ye are partakers of Christ's sufferings.'—1 *Pet.* iv. 13.

XXXI.

PAUL SET FREE.

Acts, xvi. 35 to end.

Though Paul was very happy in the jailer's house, he wanted to go and preach in other towns of Macedonia. Would God deliver him and set him free?

The morning after the terrible earthquake, some men came to the prison with a message. They asked to see the jailer, and they said to him, 'The judges desire you to let these two men go.'

The jailer must have been surprised to hear this message, for he remembered that the judges had said to him the night before, 'Keep these men safely.' What caused this change? Probably the judges had been frightened in the night by the earthquake.

The heathen thought that earthquakes showed the anger of their gods. These judges remembered how unjustly they had treated the apostles, and they hoped, if they set them free, they should not be punished by their gods, nor by the Emperor at Rome.

The jailer went and gave the message to Paul. He said, 'The judges desire me to let you go. So depart, and go in peace.'

But Paul would not go. He said, 'I am a Roman.' What did Paul mean by that? Was he not a Jew, born at Tarsus, not in Rome? Yes; but there were some men *called* Romans. It was a favour that the great Emperor at Rome gave to some men as a reward; for if a man was called a Roman, no judge could condemn him, unless he first proved him to be guilty, and called witnesses to show that he deserved punishment. All we English enjoy this privilege, but the heathen had no such privilege unless they were Romans.

M

ACTS, xvi. 39.

'And they came and besought them, and brought them out, and desired them to depart out of the city.'

The judges had condemned Paul and Silas without any trial, and the great Cæsar at Rome might have punished the judges for their behaviour. So Paul sent back this message: 'Let the judges come themselves and fetch us out.'

So the messengers went back to the judges and said, 'Those prisoners are Romans, and they say that you have beaten them openly, and that you must now come and fetch them out yourselves.'

Then the judges were frightened lest they should get into disgrace at Rome. They did not like going themselves to the prison, but to avoid disgrace they went.

How strange it must have looked to see these judges in their handsome dresses, begging the two prisoners in their poor garments to come out of the prison! They begged them not only to come out of the prison, but to leave the city as soon as they could.

The prisoners left the prison with marks of cruel stripes on their backs, but with hearts full of joy to think that the jailer had turned to God.

Where did they first go?

To the house where they had been staying before their beating and imprisonment. They went to the house of Lydia. There they found Luke and Timothy. How much grief all those friends must have felt the whole night long! But joy had come in the morning.

All the Christians in the town came to see Paul and Silas, and to hear about their imprisonment. It was sad news for them to hear that Paul and Silas must leave them; but then Luke and Timothy were to stay behind, and this must have been a great comfort.

'I bear in my body the marks of the Lord Jesus.'—*Gal.* vi. 17.

XXXII.

PAUL AT THESSALONICA.

Acts, xvii. 1–10.

Paul and Silas set out on their journey with the stripes still fresh upon their backs. In this state they travelled nearly a hundred miles.

A good road led to the largest city in Macedonia—Thessalonica. It was once built by a great general, who called it after the name of his wife, Thessalonica. The apostles must have been three days on their way.

When they arrived they found themselves in a grand city. It was close by the sea, and ships from distant countries brought many fine things to the shore. The shops were full of gay clothing, handsome furniture, and precious jewels.

There was also a synagogue in the city. Paul and Silas went there on the Sabbath, and tried to show the Jews that all the prophets had spoken of Jesus before He came into the world.

A few of the Jews believed, and they were very kind to Paul and Silas. A great many Gentiles turned from idols, and became the servants of God. Paul often went to the houses of the Christians, and taught them more about Jesus.

But he had hard work to get bread; for he did not like to ask for anything, as it would seem as if he preached for the sake of money. But he had been taught a trade when he was a boy. All young Jews were taught to make something when they were young—even those who had rich parents—for they could not tell how soon they might become poor.

Paul knew how to weave goats' hair into cloth fit for tents. In the evening Paul and Silas would begin their work, and sit up very late, that they might earn enough to buy food for the next

PAUL AT THESSALONICA. 167

day. They worked in the daytime also, when they had time. But they could hardly earn enough, and so they were very thankful when a kind friend came from Philippi with a present for them. Perhaps it was Lydia sent the present, or it might be the jailer. Very likely it was Timothy who brought it, for he soon came after Paul (though Luke did not come yet).

There were many spiteful, envious Jews at Thessalonica. They were so angry with Paul and Silas that they got a great number of bad men to come with them to seize the apostles. They heard that Paul and Silas were in the house of a good man named Jason. They came to his house, making a great noise, and they tried to break in.

Jason heard the noise, and he hid Paul and Silas. So when the riotous mob rushed into the house, Paul and Silas could not be found. Then the fierce fellows seized Jason and his friends, and brought them to the judges.

But this good Jason was not punished, for the judges let him go.

When he went home, Jason and his friends agreed together that it would be best to send away Paul and Silas that night. They were very sorry to part with them, but they feared lest the wicked people would murder the apostles if they stayed.

That very night Paul and Silas set out in the dark, intending to go to a quiet little town among the fruitful hills.

We do not know whether Timothy went with them, or whether he followed them afterwards.

The apostles, as they walked, thought of the dear Christians in Thessalonica; and prayed that they might one day see them again.

'Labouring night and day, we preached unto you the gospel of God.'—1 *Thess.* ii. 9.

XXXIII.

PAUL AT BEREA.
Acts, xvii. 10-15.

Paul and Silas had to go nearly fifty miles before they reached the quiet city among the fruitful hills. They could not walk so far in one night.

The name of the town was Berea. It was a lovely place, built on the side of a hill, among gardens, streams, and groves. It was not a place often visited by travellers, nor were there many rich people in it.

There was a synagogue in Berea. Paul and Silas went to it on the Sabbath. They must have expected to be scoffed at and contradicted: but these Jews were quite different from the Jews of Thessalonica. They listened to the preaching about Jesus, and they looked in the books of the old prophets to see what was written in them about Jesus. They found all was true that the apostles told them. In one of the books they saw it was written that Jesus would be born in Bethlehem; in another book, that 'He was led as a lamb to the slaughter.' Then Paul told them that such a Lamb was Jesus, when He was crucified for our sins.

Then many of the Jews of Berea believed in Jesus. Many of the Gentiles also believed. The apostles must have felt very happy among these believers; but they soon were made sorrowful.

The wicked Jews of Thessalonica heard that Paul was preaching at Berea. They came over the hills to Berea, for they did not care for a journey of fifty miles, if they could only hurt Paul. When they reached Berea, they tried to set the people against the apostles.

The kind Christians of Berea were

so much afraid of these wicked men, that they thought it best to send Paul quite away. Silas and Timothy were to remain at Berea, and Paul was to go away secretly, for fear any other wicked Jews should seize him by the way.

It was very sad for Paul to leave his two dear companions behind, but it was better for the Bereans that Silas and Timothy should stay.

Could Paul go quite alone upon his journey? O no! The kind Bereans would not let him go alone. Some of them went with him to the sea-shore, about ten miles off.* There they found a ship ready to sail. His kind friends went in the ship with him. They all made a long voyage, and after many days arrived at Athens,—a very grand city. Then Paul parted from his

* The words of our *version*—' *as it were* to the sea'—give the idea that Paul did not *really* go to the sea; but it means, *towards* the sea.

Berean friends, and he gave them this message to deliver to Silas and Timothy: 'Come to me very quickly.'

Paul determined to wait at Athens till they came, for he did not like to be separated long from his dear companions, though he was glad to think they were teaching the new believers at Berea. Timothy had himself been taught when a child to know the Scriptures, and he could help the Bereans to understand what the prophets had written about Jesus.

'Search the Scriptures; for in them ye think ye have eternal life: and they are they which testify of me.'—*John*, v. 39.

XXXIV.

PAUL AT ATHENS.

Acts, xvii. 16 to end.

Paul found himself alone at Athens. This was the first time he had been alone since he had begun this missionary journey.

Athens was in Greece. Paul had now left Macedonia, and had entered Greece, often called Achaia.

There was a great deal to be seen in Athens. It was the most famous city of Greece.

There never was a city with so many beautiful statues, pictures, temples, and altars. Was Paul pleased at beholding them? No; he was filled with grief, for most of the statues were the images of false gods, and all the temples were the houses of idols.

There was indeed one synagogue, where the true God was worshipped, but no place where Jesus was honoured as the Son of God. Paul went to the synagogue on the Sabbath. In the week he went to the grand market-place.

There were many wise heathens in Athens, who were always in the market-place, talking and teaching, under the shade of trees and marble colonnades. Paul went there to talk with them, and to teach them about Jesus. These pretended wise men laughed at Paul, and called him a 'babbler.' Some were offended, and said, 'He wants to set up new gods.'

But at last they proposed a plan which pleased Paul very much. These Athenians were fond of hearing new things, so they thought they should like to hear Paul preach about the new things he told them. They led him up a high hill in the city, where the judges often sat to give judgment. There were stone seats for the judges. There was a very fine temple on the hill, where Mars, the god of war, was worshipped.

Paul stood up on Mars' Hill to speak of the Prince of Peace. He spoke first of the *one* true God, who made all things; and of the sin of worshipping idols. He said God commanded them to repent, and that He would judge the world one day by the Man whom He had raised from the dead. Christ was the Man that Paul meant.

When the Athenians heard of the resurrection, some began to laugh. Others, who did not mock, said, 'We will hear about this another day.' If those people had really cared to know how to be saved, they would have wished to hear immediately, and not put off hearing till another day.

But there were a few who really believed in Jesus. One of them was a wise and great man—even a judge. Another was a lady.

The Lord did not wish Paul to stay

at Athens, where there were so many mockers. It is seldom that mockers get any good to their souls. It is a very great sin to mock at holy words, Many have lost heaven by a mocking spirit.

'How long, ye simple ones, will ye love simplicity? and the scorners delight in their scorning?'— *Prov.* i. 22.

XXXV.

PAUL AT CORINTH.

Acts, xviii. 1–5.

THE Lord showed Paul when he ought to leave a city, and where he ought to go. Paul did not stay long among the scoffers of Athens; for he could do more good in other cities. He set out on his journey, meaning to go to a very large city about fifty miles off.

His way lay by the sea-coast. There was the great sea on each side of him, as he travelled alone to Corinth.

Corinth was a far richer city than Athens. It was now the capital of Greece. The chief pleasure in Athens was to talk about new things; but the chief pleasure at Corinth was to feast, and dance, and play at games. Once in three years people came from far countries to Corinth to see the games. At these games men ran races, and wrestled together, and threw spears, and hurled stones, and leaped over fences.

In Corinth there were many gluttons and drunkards, many disorderly people, and many vain, foolish women. But there were not as many learned people, or as many scoffers, as in Athens.

When Paul arrived there, he looked out for a lodging.

He found two people who were tentmakers, as he was. He thought it would be convenient to live with those of the same trade as himself. These two people were travellers like Paul, and they were also of the same nation. Aquila was a Jew, and his wife Priscilla was a Jewess. Paul sat with them and wove his goats' hair into coarse cloth, close by their sides. As they worked they talked. What did Paul talk about? His Saviour.

Aquila and Priscilla had not believed in Jesus crucified for their sins, till Paul told them the wonderful story. But when they did hear about Him, they believed in Him, and they tried to please Him in everything.

Every Sabbath, Paul went to the synagogue and showed that Jesus was the Christ—the promised Saviour. Aquila and Priscilla heard Paul preach at the synagogue, and they listened very earnestly.

PAUL AT CORINTH.

One day Paul had the delight of seeing again his dearest friends, Silas and Timothy. They were just come from Macedonia. Perhaps you wonder they had not come to Paul while he was at Athens. They did come while Paul was at Athens, but he had sent them back to Macedonia, and now they came to Corinth.

It was not their fault that they had not come sooner. Paul had written to them to bid them teach the new Christians at Thessalonica, and other places, as he was afraid the new Christians might turn back to Satan.*

How glad he was to see his dear son Timothy again! He was more glad when he heard good accounts of the believers in Macedonia. He sat down one night, and instead of working at his loom and weaving the goats' hair, he took his pen and began to write on

* 'We thought it good to be left at Athens alone, and sent Timotheus our brother.... lest by some means the tempter have tempted you.'—1 *Thess.* iii. 1-7.

parchment a letter to the believers at Thessalonica. This letter is in the Bible, and is called 'The First Epistle of Paul to the Thessalonians.' There were no postmen in those days to take letters, and Paul sent it by the hand of the first faithful messenger he could find.

After this time Paul wrote a great many letters, and some of them we can read in our Bibles. He did not write all these letters with his own hand, but he asked his friends to write for him.

At the time that Silas and Timothy arrived the apostle was in want of food. Though he worked so hard he could not earn enough to support him, for there was a famine in the land, and the price of food was six times as much as usual.

But did not the Corinthians give him anything?

Paul would not accept any presents from them, because he knew they would be ready to say he preached in order to get money.

Silas and Timothy brought in their hands presents from Philippi—perhaps from Lydia and the jailer.*

The Philippians were the most generous of all the people to whom Paul preached, and they were the only people who sent him presents in his distress. Paul was very grateful for their kindness.†

Now we may think of the five friends sitting together at night—Paul, Silas, Timothy, Aquila, and Priscilla—all busy at their work, and singing praises to Jesus.

'In weariness and painfulness, in watchings often, in hunger and thirst.'—2 *Cor.* xi. 27.

* 'When I was present with you and *wanted* . . . . that which was lacking to me the brethren which came from Macedonia supplied.'—2 *Cor.* xi. 9–12.

† 'Ye Philippians . . . . when I departed from Macedonia, no church communicated with me . . . but ye only.'—*Philip.* iv. 15.

XXXVI.

END OF PAUL'S SECOND MISSIONARY JOURNEY.

Acts, xviii. 7–22.

You have heard that Paul was much comforted by the arrival of Silas and Timothy. He was more earnest than ever to preach Jesus in the synagogue. But he could only persuade a few Jews to believe on Him, as the Son of God.

Most of the Jews grew more and more angry. At last Paul shook his clothes in their sight, and said, that if they perished he was clear of their blood. 'From this time I will go to the Gentiles.' So he went no more to the synagogue, but he did not leave the city. All that believed in Jesus came to hear Paul in a house close by. This house belonged to a good man named Justus.

Among the believers who came to

this house was the chief ruler of the synagogue, a man named Crispus. Who would have expected that the chief ruler of the synagogue should believe? All the family of Crispus believed, as well as himself, and they were all baptized by Paul.

A great many more people believed and were baptized. Soon there was quite a large congregation meeting in the house of Justus.

But the unbelieving Jews were enraged at seeing so many believe, and Paul feared he should be seized, and beaten, and imprisoned.

However, at night he had a dream that cheered him much. The Lord appeared to him, and said, 'Be not afraid, but speak, and do not be silent; for I AM WITH THEE, and no man shall set on thee to hurt thee; for I have much people in this city.'

Now Paul knew that many people would turn to the Lord, and that no one would hurt him. He stayed in Corinth a year and a half, and went on teaching the Word.

At this time a new governor came to Corinth. His name was Gallio. The Jews seized Paul and dragged him before the governor. 'What has he done?' asked Gallio. The Jews replied, 'He has been teaching us to worship God in a wrong way.'

Paul was just going to open his mouth to defend himself, when Gallio cried out, 'If this man had *done* anything wicked I would have judged him, but as it is only about what he *says*, I will not hear you.' The Jews did not like this answer, and wanted to speak more. But Gallio drove them out. 'Go away! go away!' said he. So Paul was set free. In this way God kept His promise that no one should hurt him.

After a good while, Paul said he should leave Corinth. He could not always stay in one place, as he must preach the Gospel to many heathen nations. Priscilla and Aquila also wanted to go away.

The five friends agreed to sail in the ship.

The first place the ship stopped at was Cenchrea. Paul landed there to have his hair and beard shorn, for he had made the Nazarite's vow a month before. That vow was not to drink wine, nor to be shorn, for a month.* He made the vow when delivered from the Jews at Gallio's judgment-seat. He wished to show the Jews that he kept their customs, though he trusted in Jesus for salvation.

There was a good woman at Cenchrea, named Phœbe, who received him, and was kind to him while at

* See Num. vi. for an account of the Nazarite's vow. Samson and Samuel, and John the Baptist, were Nazarites.

Cenchrea. She was ready to help all the Christians she saw.*

Then Paul returned to the ship and crossed the sea, till he came to Asia. He stopped near a fine city called Ephesus. It was the grandest city in all Asia, with the most splendid temple ever built in honour of an idol. At this grand city Priscilla and Aquila said they must stay and live. Paul and his other companions just landed and rested there for a few days.

Paul preached in the synagogue. The Jews liked what he said so much that they begged him to stay, but Paul told them he could not, as he was hastening to Jerusalem to keep one of the holy feasts. 'But,' said Paul, 'I will return to you if God will.'

So, bidding farewell to Priscilla and Aquila, and the kind Ephesians, Paul and his companions set sail again.

* 'Phœbe, our sister, she hath been a succourer of many.'—*Rom.* xvi. 1. 2.

He landed at Cæsarea, and went up to Jerusalem. He saw his friends there, and worshipped the Lord in His holy city. It must have been delightful to relate his wonderful history to any apostles who were there. But he did not stay long; he hastened back to Antioch in Syria, the city from which he had set out several years ago.

Thus ended his *second* missionary journey. It had been indeed a blessed journey, for thousands of heathens had turned to God. In this journey the Gospel was first preached in Europe, for Macedonia and Greece are in Europe.

'Unto me .... is this grace given, that I should preach among the Gentiles the unsearchable riches of Christ.'—*Eph*. iii. 8.

XXXVII.

THE ELOQUENT PREACHER.

Acts, xviii. 24 to end.

LEAVING Paul at Antioch in Syria, let us go back to Ephesus in Asia.

Soon after Paul left Ephesus, a new preacher appeared at the synagogue. He was a Jew, born in Egypt, who travelled about, and was just come from Rome. Aquila and Priscilla listened to him, and were much struck, for he was very eloquent; that is, he spoke in beautiful language, and very earnestly. He knew the Old Testament well; he could refer to the prophecies and explain their meaning. He knew even more than this, (for many Jews knew the Old Testament); he knew the preaching of John the Baptist,—what he said about repentance, and about baptism, and the coming of Jesus; but here he stopped. He knew

THE ELOQUENT PREACHER. 189

not that Jesus had been crucified, and risen again, and had sent down the Holy Ghost upon believers.

Aquila and Priscilla listened attentively, and they were sorry to find Apollos did not know about Jesus; so they got him to come to them, and they told him all about His sacrifice for our sins. How did they know about these things? Paul had instructed them while they were sitting weaving together.

This preacher's name was Apollos. You see he was a very humble man, for he was willing to listen, even to a woman, when he found Priscilla could teach him about Jesus.

He wished very much to go into Greece, that he might preach in the synagogues, for whenever he preached many came to hear him on account of his eloquence. But he was afraid the brethren in Greece would not know he was a Christian, and would not receive him.

Aquila, Priscilla, and others, said they would write letters to the Christians they knew in Greece. In these letters they said Apollos was a good man, and knew about Jesus; and they said, 'Pray receive and listen to him.'

So Apollos took these letters and showed them to the Christians in Greece, and then he preached in the synagogues. The believers were much comforted by all he said. When he preached he showed the Jews what the prophets had said about Jesus in the Scriptures; and he convinced a great many.

The chief cities in Greece, or Achaia, were Corinth and Athens.

The first city in Greece where Apollos preached was Corinth. He heard at Corinth a great deal about Paul, but he had not yet seen him, for Paul was still at Antioch in Syria.

Would not Paul be glad to hear that another preacher was teaching his converts at Corinth more about Jesus?

'Who then is Paul, and who is Apollos, but ministers by whom ye believed?'—1 *Cor.* iii. 5.

XXXVIII.

PAUL'S THIRD MISSIONARY JOURNEY.

Acts, xviii. 22, 23.

WE have now read of two missionary journeys. The first when Paul set out with Barnabas and Mark. The second when he set out with Silas. From both these journeys he had returned safely, after suffering many afflictions.

Would Paul take a third missionary journey?

Yes, he would, for it was his chief delight to tell the heathen about Jesus.

He spent some time at Antioch with

the brethren, and then he set out again. Whom did he take with him on this third journey?

One of his companions was a young man named Titus. He was a Greek. His native city was Corinth, the capital of Greece, or Achaia. Paul loved Titus much, and called him his son. It seems he loved Timothy still more, for he called him his dearly-beloved son. We are not sure whether Timothy set out on this journey with Paul. Silas was left behind at Jerusalem, as we think. Some Macedonians may have accompanied him, but we are not sure of their names.

Where did Paul and Titus go?

They went through Little Asia. This Little Asia was divided into provinces. One was called Cilicia. Tarsus was in Cilicia. There Paul was born; his relations lived there. It is probable Paul visited his native city.

He went afterwards into a province

called Galatia. There were wild, warm-hearted people, who lived in it. Paul had visited Galatia some years before. The people were very fond of Paul at first, till false teachers came and set them against him for a time.

But they readily granted Paul's request. What was it? He had promised the brethren, that he would collect money for the poor saints in Jerusalem, who were in great distress. You remember there was a famine in most lands, and besides the famine there were persecutions at Jerusalem, so the poor saints were often in great distress.

When Paul left Galatia he went to other parts of Asia, and visited Lystra, which was dear to him as Timothy's birth-place. We know not whether Timothy's pious mother, Eunice, was still living.

Paul went through the province of Phrygia, and then went down towards the great city of Ephesus. When he had landed there on his last journey he had promised to return soon, and now he had come; *not* by *sea*, as before, but by *land*. He found there many believers, and amongst them Aquila and Priscilla, his old friends, whom he had left there at his last visit.

It was a great joy to meet them again. Paul could sit with them as he used, and weave goats' hair into cloth for tents. Thus he earned bread for himself and his companions, and he gave to the poor all he could spare.

Timothy was now with him, and Titus was with him still, and the believers who had followed him from Macedonia. Very happy was this party of Christians. In the evening while they wove cloth, they would talk about the labours of the day, and praise God for the blessing He gave to their words.

'These hands have ministered

unto my necessities, and to them that were with me.'—*Acts*, xx. 34.

XXXIX.

THE DISCIPLES OF JOHN THE BAPTIST AT EPHESUS.

Acts, xix. 1–12.

When Paul arrived at Ephesus, he did not find Apollos there. That eloquent preacher had gone to Corinth a long while before, and was still there. It must have disappointed Paul not to see him.

But there were twelve men at Ephesus, very much like Apollos in not knowing about Jesus, but they had not met with any such teachers as Apollos had found. Why had not Aquila and Priscilla taught them? Perhaps these twelve men had not preached, and so their ignorance had not been seen.

Paul began to talk to these twelve men. He found they believed in the true God, and in the Old Testament, and in the preaching of the Baptist—but that was all. They did not know about the resurrection of Jesus. Paul said to them, 'Have ye received the Holy Ghost since ye believed?' They replied, 'We never heard of the Holy Ghost.' Perhaps they meant that they had never heard of the Holy Ghost being given at Pentecost. 'Unto what, then, were you baptized?' inquired Paul. 'We were baptized unto John's baptism,' answered the twelve. Paul then said, 'John verily baptized with the baptism of repentance, telling the people they should believe on Him who should come after him, that is, on Christ Jesus.'

'When they heard this they were baptized in the name of the Lord Jesus.'

Thus these men were twice baptized. Afterwards Paul laid his hands on them. Then the Holy Ghost was given to them, and they began to speak in various tongues and to prophesy. You remember that none but apostles could bestow these wonderful gifts.

Then Paul appeared again in the synagogue. Those who liked to hear Paul preach, when he paid his first short visit, must have been glad to see him enter the synagogue again. But they liked him less when they heard him boldly declare Jesus to be the only Saviour. They contradicted him, and made objections to all he said.

Paul went on preaching there for three months. At last he could not go any more to the synagogue, for the Jews tried to set the people against the way of salvation by Jesus.

When Paul departed from the synagogue, a man, named Tyrannus, lent him a large room, in which wise men used to give lectures about worldly knowledge. Perhaps this Tyrannus was converted, but we know not his motive for lending this room. Paul invited people to come there every day to be taught, and many came.

This teaching went on for two years, and all that lived in Ephesus, and in other cities, heard the word of the Lord Jesus—Jews as well as Greeks.

And God enabled Paul to do very great miracles. Not only did he cure sick people when he saw them, and touched them, and spake to them,— but he did still more. If Paul touched a handkerchief or apron, and it was brought to a sick person, he was made well by touching it, or, if he had an evil spirit, the poor creature was delivered from it. Just as people who have fevers and plagues give their diseases to others, if healthy people touch clothes they have touched; so the body of this apostle could give health to the sick and afflicted, by clothes that he had touched being sent to them. It was Christ's promise that His apostles should do greater works than He had done.

'He that believeth on me, the works that I do shall he do also; and greater works than these shall he do; because I go unto my Father.'—*John*, xiv. 12.

XL.

PAUL'S MEETING WITH APOLLOS.

Various passages in the two Epistles to the Corinthians.

At last Paul had the comfort and delight of seeing Apollos. He had heard much of him, and now he saw that eloquent man and blessed preacher. Apollos came to Ephesus while Paul was still there. He had just come from Corinth, the capital of Greece. He had a great deal to tell Paul about the Corinthians—some good, but more evil.

Paul was made so uneasy by hearing of their sins, that he went over the sea that he might reprove the offenders.

He stayed at Corinth a very short time, and was much grieved to find that Apollos' account was only too true. There were many there very fond of Apollos, who said, 'I am of Apollos;' others who said, 'I am of Paul;' yet they did not follow what Apollos taught or what Paul taught.

Paul soon returned to Ephesus. He thought it would be best to send some good men to Corinth, that they might bring the Corinthians to repentance. He fixed upon Timothy as one messenger, and on Erastus as another (a man born in Corinth). He told them to go round by Macedonia, and to collect money for the poor saints in Jerusalem as they passed through Philippi, Thessalonica, and Berea.

While the messengers were absent Paul wrote a letter to the Corinthians. He wrote it with many tears, caused by the anguish of his heart. This pain was worse to him than all the labour of his hands to earn bread.

When he had finished his very long letter he sent it by Titus, who was a native of Corinth. Titus was afraid lest he should be ill received by the sinful Christians at Corinth. But Titus obeyed Paul's wishes, and went with a companion to Corinth. He took Trophimus as his companion.

When Titus arrived at Corinth he was received most affectionately. The Corinthians were quite penitent, and ready to obey Titus in everything. Paul's letter was read to them, and it made a great impression: for the Corinthians attended more to what Paul *wrote* than to what he *spoke*, for he was not a fine speaker, nor was he grand-looking.

Titus did not soon come back to Ephesus. Paul continued to feel great anxiety about the Corinthians, and kept longing for Titus's return.

'Titus is my partner and fellow-helper concerning you.'—2 *Cor.* viii. 23.

XLI.

THE SORCERERS.

Acts, xix. 13–20.

As Athens was famous for learning, as Corinth was famous for games, so Ephesus was for sorcery. The city of Ephesus was full of deceivers. The devil had great power in Ephesus, and enabled people to deceive others by their pretended wonders.

These deceivers were called sorcerers, or wizards, or magicians, or charmers, or exorcists. These names all mean the same thing.

When these sorcerers heard of Paul's miracles, they tried to do miracles of their own. There was one old man named Sceva. He was a Jew, and he was a chief priest. He had seven sons, and he ought to have brought them all up to serve the God of Israel.

But these seven sons served the devil. They wanted to do the same miracles that Paul did, without believing in Jesus.

There was a man who had a very fierce evil spirit. The seven brothers went to his house to cast out the evil spirit. They stood over him and said, 'I command thee by Jesus whom Paul preaches to come out of him.'

The evil spirit, instead of coming out of the man, made this terrible answer,—'Jesus I know, and Paul I know; but who are you?'

Having said this, the man jumped up suddenly, seized hold of the brothers, struggled with all seven of them, tore their clothes, and bruised their bodies, and conquered them; so that the frightened brothers ran from the house with hardly any clothes, and many bleeding wounds.

This overthrow of the sorcerers was much talked of by the people of Ephesus; and it made many praise the Lord Jesus by whom Paul did such real wonders.

There were many other sorcerers in Ephesus, who came to Paul and confessed the wicked tricks they had played through Satan; and they brought their books about their charms and burned them in the streets before all the people. They would not sell the books, because they were wicked books. They might have got fifty thousand pieces of silver* for them if they had sold them, but they loved Jesus more than silver.

Many more people believed in Jesus

* A piece of silver is worth tenpence.

when they saw the burning of the books.

'*Sorcerers*, and idolaters, and all liars, shall have their part in the lake which burneth with fire and brimstone.'—*Rev.* xxi. 8.

XLII.

THE UPROAR AT EPHESUS.

Acts, xix. 23 to end.

In the city of Ephesus there was an immense and beautiful temple—the finest idol temple in the world. It was built of white marble, and it was surrounded by green marble pillars. But to whose honour was it built?

To the honour of an ugly idol called Diana. There are many beautiful statues called Diana; but this idol was a mere block of wood, with something like a head at the top, and short arms at the sides, leaning on two iron sticks to keep it from falling. This block was adorned with a splendid crown and girdle, and carefully preserved behind a rich curtain, in a kind of little temple in the midst of the great temple. The priests who waited on the idol taught the people that it came down from heaven.

People came from all countries to worship Diana, and to join in her riotous feasts, and they used to carry little shrines to their children at home, as a remembrance of her. These shrines were made of silver, and were like little temples with the idol inside.

There was a man named Demetrius; he had grown rich by making these silver shrines. He found that people did not buy so many as they used. He knew that Paul had turned multitudes from the worship of idols. This made him very angry, for he felt that he should not get so much money by his shrines.

He wished to stop Paul from preaching.

The way he took was to call together all the silversmiths in the place and to make them a speech.

In his speech he told them, that Paul was turning every one away from their great goddess Diana, and that they should soon have no more shrines to make.

The silversmiths were so much enraged that they began to cry out with all their might, 'Great is Diana of the Ephesians!'

The people in the city heard the cry and seized two of Paul's companions, called Gaius and Aristarchus. The people then dragged them into a large place called a theatre.

Paul heard the uproar, and wanted to go into the theatre after his companions, but the Christians in Ephesus would not let him go in, lest he should be torn to pieces.

It was one of the amusements in this theatre to see wild beasts tear each other to pieces. Who could say what those fierce men might do to Paul?

For two hours the people continued to cry out, 'Great is Diana of the Ephesians!'

At last a chief man of the city rose up and spoke.

The riotous bawlers stopped when they saw him. He spoke to them very wisely, and advised them to be quiet, and to go home.

What a comfort it was when this uproar ceased! and those two friends, Gaius and Aristarchus, who had been dragged into the theatre, had not been torn to pieces by the furious mob!

This was God's deliverance of His own servants from men more cruel than wild beasts.

'I have fought with beasts at Ephesus.'—1 *Cor.* xv. 32.

XLIII.

THE COMING OF TITUS.

Acts, xx. 1-6.

AFTER the uproar was over at Ephesus Paul prepared to leave the place, for it was dangerous to remain.

He called all the believers together, and took leave of them with much affection. He had been much shaken by the uproar, and had almost died from fear and trembling.*

Then he set out with his own companions. Their names are not mentioned in the Scriptures. Timothy was not one of them, for he was gone on before to the very country where Paul was now going. What was that country? The country to which the man in the dream had called him long ago—Macedonia.

* 2 Cor. i. 8.

On the way to Macedonia, Paul went to Troas, hoping there to meet Titus.

Day after day he waited there, but he was cast down by Titus not arriving. Why was he so anxious? He wanted to know whether the Corinthians had minded the letter he had sent by Titus. He feared lest they were going on in their sinful ways.

Wearied of waiting for Titus at Troas, Paul set out for Macedonia, hoping to meet him there. He went to that city of Macedonia where he had first preached the gospel—Philippi. There he saw friends who had often sent him presents in his distress. Lydia may have been one of those friends, and the jailer another.

But he did not find Titus there. At last the much-longed-for one came. After Paul had been waiting some time, Titus arrived with most joyful news. The Corinthians had repented. So Paul wrote them a comforting letter,

THE COMING OF TITUS.

and sent it by the hands of Titus. That young minister's heart now burned with affection for the Corinthians, and he gladly went back to Corinth with Paul's letter of forgiveness.

Paul now travelled about Greece, and to other countries beyond, still collecting for the saints at Jerusalem. He was accompanied by many brethren. At length he determined to visit Jerusalem, and he set sail with many companions, and landed at Troas, on the way to Jerusalem.

'Exceedingly the more joyed we for the joy of Titus, because his spirit was refreshed by you all.'—2 *Cor.* vii. 13.

XLIV.

THE SLEEPY HEARER.
Acts, xx. 7–13.

There were eight brethren now assembled with Paul at Troas (amongst them were Luke and Timothy). Paul spent a week at Troas.

The last day of his stay was Saturday. The Jewish Sabbath was over on Saturday evening.

On that evening all the Christians met together in an upper chamber on the third floor. There were many lights in it. A young man, named Eutychus, sat near a large window that was open. Paul preached a great while, even till midnight, and the young man fell asleep. In his sleep he fell out of window. The little congregation saw him fall, and they rushed down the stairs outside, going through the window. Paul stopped preaching, and went down also. All the Christians

ACTS, xx. 12.
'And they brought the young man alive, and were not a little comforted.'

were much grieved to find the youth lying dead upon the ground.

But Paul stretched himself over the body, and held it in his arms, and said to the weeping friends, 'Do not be grieved, for his life is in him.' The young man was indeed alive, and his friends were comforted. They all went up again with Paul.

It was now past midnight, so it was Sunday morning. During the dark hours of the morning the happy Christians broke bread, in remembrance of their crucified Lord ; and they talked about Him a long while. When the beams of the rising sun shone upon them, Paul and his eight companions took leave of their fellow-Christians, and left Troas. The eight companions went down to the ship and set sail, but Paul preferred walking alone.

' God, which raiseth the dead.' —2 *Cor.* i. 9.

XLV.

PAUL'S FAREWELL TO THE EPHESIANS.

Acts, xx. 13 to end.

PAUL's companions got into a ship, while Paul himself walked across the land, about twenty miles. The way was through groves of oak-trees, which shaded the apostle from the sun, while the little birds on this spring day filled the air with their warblings.

Why did Paul wish to go this day's journey all alone? How gladly would Luke, or Timothy, or any of the brethren, have walked with him! No doubt he wished to speak as he went along to his Father in heaven. Had not his God that very night enabled him to revive the dead?

He found the ship at the place he had fixed upon. That place was Assos. He got into the ship, and he sailed away in it.

PAUL'S FAREWELL.

As the ship did not belong to Paul, he could not make it stop where he pleased. He would have liked the ship to stop at Ephesus, but it sailed past that great city, and stopped at Miletus.

When Paul heard that the ship would stay some time at that place, he sent a message to Ephesus to ask the chief ministers or elders to come and see him. The messengers had thirty miles to go. But these Ephesians loved Paul so much that they quickly came to him. They saw again their beloved apostle, and they saw also two of their own countrymen who had travelled with him by sea and land, named Tychicus and Trophimus. Paul spoke to them in a most affectionate manner. He told them he was going to Jerusalem, and that he knew that he should be put in prison. 'But,' said he, 'I am ready to give up my life for Jesus.' Then he said, 'I know that you shall see my face no more.'

He reminded them how he had taught them night and day for three years, and how with his own hands he had earned his bread. Then he kneeled down and prayed with them all. They all wept very bitterly, and fell on Paul's neck and kissed him. What grieved them most was Paul's saying that they should see his face no more. Their love to him was very great. They would not leave him till they saw him get into the ship and sail away. They had a long journey home, and they must have shed many tears by the way.

'Neither count I my life dear unto myself, so that I might finish my course with joy.'—*Acts*, xx. 24.

ACTS, xx. 37.
'And they all wept sore, and fell on Paul's neck, and kissed him.'

XLVI.

PAUL'S VISIT TO PHILIP.

Acts, xxi. 1-14.

Paul went sailing on, first in one ship and then in another, till he came to the city of Tyre. That city is just above the land of Canaan, and from it a poor woman once came to ask mercy of the Lord Jesus when on earth.

The ship stopped here to unload, for it was filled with good things for the people of Tyre to buy. We do not know for certain what they were; very likely sacks of wheat and barrels of wine from the fruitful fields of Asia.

Paul and his companions landed, and spent seven days with the Christians of Tyre. That woman who had so much faith in Jesus must often have talked of her beloved Lord, but perhaps she was dead now.

Among the Christians of Tyre there were some prophets, and they told Paul that if he went up to Jerusalem he should have much sorrow; but Paul would go, for he was ready to suffer for Jesus' sake.

When the week was over, Paul and his companions walked towards the sea-shore. The Christians of Tyre walked with them, and even their children. When they were out of the city they all kneeled down on the sea-shore and prayed. Would the children ever forget seeing Paul go away? There was an affectionate parting by the side of the ship. The Christians from Tyre went home.

Soon the ship came to the end of its voyage, just at the foot of Mount Carmel—that mount where long ago Elijah had prayed for fire to consume the sacrifice.

The ship went no further. Paul and his companions continued their

ACTS, XXI. 5.

'And they all brought us on our way, with wives and children, till we were out of the city; and we kneeled down on the shore, and prayed.'

journey on foot along the sea-coast. They went thirty-five miles, and then came to the fine city of Cæsarea. *There* once lived Cornelius, the Roman centurion—the first Gentile who received the Holy Ghost from heaven. That was more than twenty years ago. Probably he was not there, for soldiers do not remain long in one place.

But one old man was there whom Paul had seen. Yes! he had seen him once in Jerusalem, when Stephen was stoned.* This old man was Philip the deacon. He was one of the seven deacons, Stephen was another. This deacon had once been sent to talk to the rich Ethiopian in his chariot, some twenty years ago.

Philip was still at Cæsarea. He was living there with his four daughters. They were all prophetesses. It was indeed a holy family—such a father and such daughters!

---

* He had seen him since, probably. (Acts, xviii. 22.)

Paul liked to stay in the house of this good man. His companions stayed there, too. Some of them *may* have left him, but of this we are sure, Luke was with him, and the two Ephesians, Tychicus and Trophimus.

There came one day to Philip's house a prophet, named Agabus. He took off Paul's long girdle and bound his own hands and feet with it. What could he mean by this? Paul must have wondered. He said, 'So shall the Jews at Jerusalem bind the man that weareth this girdle; and they shall deliver him to the Gentiles.'

When Paul's friends heard these words they began to entreat him not to go to Jerusalem. Luke and Philip and all the rest joined in the entreaty, while they shed many tears. Paul answered, 'Why do you weep and break my heart? for I am ready not only to be bound, but to die in Jerusalem for the Lord Jesus.'

When his friends could not persuade him they left off begging him, saying, 'The will of the Lord be done!'

Then Paul and his companions went on, walking to Jerusalem.

'For me to live is Christ, and to die is gain.'—*Philip.* i. 21.

XLVII.

JOY IN JERUSALEM.

Acts, xxi. 15-19.

PAUL left Cæsarea with more companions than he brought with him. Christians loved Paul, and liked to be with him. They wanted also to keep the Feast of Pentecost at Jerusalem.

The distance was seventy-five miles, which must have taken them three days to travel.

They had to pack up their luggage* to send by some way to Jerusalem. They had also much money to take to the poor saints in that city.

Their journey must have been hot, for it was now summer, and what we call Whitsuntide.

When they arrived at Jerusalem they went to the house of a very good old man, who had long believed in Jesus.†

The brethren in Jerusalem were very glad to see this famous apostle Paul. Luke, also, they must have been glad to see, for he had already written his precious history of Jesus.

We do not know how many apostles

---

* The word translated 'carriages' means 'luggage.' (Acts, xxi. 15.)

† This Mnason lived in Jerusalem, and those disciples who knew Mnason led Paul and Luke, and their companions, to the house of this good old man. Instead of the words, 'They brought with them one Mnason,' these words ought to have been put, 'They led them to one Mnason, with whom they lodged.' (Acts xxi. 16.)

there were now at Jerusalem. One there certainly was, James. He was the ruler of the Christians in Jerusalem.

Paul knew they wished to hear about his travels, and he related how God had turned the hearts of many Gentiles from idols to Jesus.

The brethren were all delighted to hear this account; and they praised God for His wonderful works. Paul gave them also the money for the poor saints—the gift of the Gentiles.

This was a joyful beginning. But soon all that the Holy Spirit had said by the prophet came true.

' As touching brotherly love, ye need not that I write unto you: for ye yourselves are taught of God to love one another.'—1 *Thess.* iv. 9.

XLVIII.

THE UPROAR IN THE TEMPLE.

Acts, xxi. 18–33.

The day after Paul's arrival a great meeting was held in Jerusalem. The apostle James was chief over the assembly: many elders were there. Christians brought large sums of money, collected in distant countries, for the poor saints in Jerusalem.

When they had presented these gifts, Paul began to address the assembly.

He told them the history of his travels, and of the conversions the Lord had wrought among the Gentiles. What praises flowed from the lips of the believers, when Paul had finished his speech!

Then some elders arose and began to give the apostles their advice. What, did they think that Paul needed their advice? Yes, they did. They had met with Jews who bore false witness of Paul, and who said he set people against the law of Moses. Was this true?

Then they gave this advice. 'Brother, show that you honour the law of Moses by doing what we desire. We have here four men who have made a vow (probably the vow of the Nazarite); see that they shave their heads, and let them purify themselves with you, and do you pay the expenses. Thus you will show thousands of Jews that you keep the law, and teach the Jews to keep it.'

Paul followed this advice. He took the men into the Temple, for they were Jews.

Did this satisfy the fierce Jews? No, it only made Paul's accusers more violent.

The men were purified during seven days. When the seven days were almost over, some Jews from Asia (probably from the city of Ephesus), seeing Paul in the Temple, stirred up the people against him, and seized him, saying, 'This Paul is the man who goes about speaking against the Temple; and he has now taken Gentiles into the Temple.'

Paul had never done this. These wicked Jews had seen him walking in the streets with Trophimus the Ephesian; but Paul had never taken him into the Temple.

But most people believed what the Jews from Asia said; and they all ran together into the Temple. They found Paul in the court of Israel, near the altar (where he had a right to be). They seized hold of him, and dragged him out of the court, down the steps. The Levites shut the great brass doors behind him. His enemies hurried him into the streets, and would soon have stoned him,—as they had stoned Stephen more than twenty years before,—had they not been suddenly stopped in their wickedness.

There was a great tower just above the Temple, where a thousand Roman soldiers lodged. The captain heard that there was an uproar in the city, and he ran down in haste, with many soldiers, to the place where Paul was. He found the Jews beating him, but when these men saw the captain they left off beating Paul; for they knew they had no right to do so.

The chief captain came near and desired his soldiers to bind Paul between two, with two chains (as Peter had once been bound).

Now the prophecies about Paul began to come true. Here is Paul in chains. Will he not soon be in prison? May he not soon be led forth to die?

'The Holy Ghost witnesseth in every city, saying that bonds and afflictions abide me.'—*Acts*, xx. 23.

XLIX.

THE UPROAR ON THE CASTLE STAIRS.

Acts, xxi. 33 to end; xxii. 1–23.

When the captain had bound Paul, he inquired what he had done to make the people so angry with him.

The people gave so many answers to this question that the captain did not know what to believe. Some cried out one thing and some another, and there was such confusion that the captain desired the soldiers to take him into the tower, or castle.

The soldiers led him along till they came to the stairs up to the castle. As they went up those stairs the people pushed the soldiers so much that Paul was lifted off his feet and carried up the stairs in the soldiers' arms. All the time the people, who were pressing up the stairs, kept on crying out, 'Away with him!' These people were ferocious

ACTS, xxi. 40.

'Paul stood on the stairs, and beckoned with the hand unto the people.'

as hounds ready to seize upon a harmless deer.

The captain had gone up the stairs first, for as Paul was on his way he saw the captain, and very respectfully said to him, 'May I speak unto the people?'

The captain wanted to know who he was. Paul answered, 'I am a Jew of Tarsus, and I beseech thee suffer me to speak unto the people.' Then the captain gave leave for his prisoner to speak.

Then Paul stood on the stairs, rather near the top, and made a sign to the people below that he was going to speak.

The fierce multitude wanted to hear him speak, wondering what he would say; and so they suddenly became quite silent.

Then Paul spoke. He told the multitude his history—how he once cruelly treated the Christians—and how he saw a light from heaven, and heard Jesus speak—and how he was made blind—and how Ananias restored his sight—and how he preached about Jesus in Jerusalem, till God said, 'Depart, I will send thee far away to the Gentiles.'

As soon as Paul had uttered these words, there arose such cries and shouts from the people beneath as you never heard. Amidst their yells they screamed, 'Away with such a fellow from the earth; for it is not fit that he should live!' As they cried out, they took off their upper garments to prepare for stoning him, and they threw dust in the air, in their rage.

'Forbidding us to speak to the Gentiles that they might be saved.'—1 *Thess.* ii. 16.

L.

PAUL'S ESCAPE FROM SCOURGING.

Acts, xxii. 24–29.

The captain began to think that Paul must have committed some very dreadful crime to make the Jews so angry with him. So he desired a centurion to take him into the castle, and to have him scourged till he would confess what he had done. What a horrible command this was! For what crime could Paul confess? He might have died under the scourge before he could confess. But Paul remembered that he was a Roman; that is, he had the privileges of a Roman citizen, though he was a Jew.

That privilege was—not to be punished without being tried first, and found guilty. What was thought so great a privilege in those countries, is now enjoyed by every Englishman. No one can be punished, unless found guilty.

The soldiers were binding Paul with straps of leather to the whipping-post, before they beat him with rods, and the centurion was standing near; when Paul said to the centurion, 'Is it lawful for you to scourge a man who is a Roman, and who has not been condemned?'

When the centurion heard this, he told the soldiers not to go on with their work, and he went to the captain and said, 'You must take care what you do, for this man is a Roman.'

Then the captain was quite frightened at having bound him with straps or thongs, and he went quickly to Paul, and said, 'Tell me, art thou a Roman?'

Paul said, 'Yes.'

The captain said, 'I paid a great deal of money to be made a Roman.'

'But *I*,' said Paul, 'was free-born.' He meant that his father had the privilege, and so he, his son, inherited it from him.

The captain then sent away the

soldiers, and made them put away their straps and their rods.

But he thought it best to let Paul sleep in the castle that night, for had he sent him back, the Jews might have torn him in pieces.

So Paul slept that night in the castle. But he was not treated as a common prisoner, because he was a Roman. Yet he still wore his chains, for even a Roman might wear chains.*

But what a night his friends must have passed in the city beneath! How sorrowful Trophimus must have felt, and Timothy, and Luke—not knowing what their dear friend and father might be suffering!

'And the Lord shall deliver me from every evil work.'—2 *Tim.* iv. 18.

* A Roman might be bound with a chain, and beaten with a staff; but he might not be bound with *thongs* and beaten with *rods*.

LI.

A JOYFUL NIGHT IN THE CASTLE.

Acts, xxii. 30 ; xxiii. 1–11.

The captain was very anxious to do what was right to Paul as a Roman citizen. He thought it would be best to let his own nation judge him. So he sent a message to the councillors of the Sanhedrim to come to their hall in the morning.

The seventy-two judges assembled early in their judgment-hall.

The soldiers took off Paul's chains, and brought him down and placed him before the judgment-seat. The Sanhedrim had left off meeting in the Temple court; they now met in another place outside the court. The Roman soldiers were allowed to enter that place, as it was not sacred.

Paul stood before the council, and looked at them earnestly. He knew many of them, for he himself had once belonged to the council, and had helped in condemning Stephen.

His first words were—'Men and brethren, I have lived before God as my conscience showed me was right.'

The high priest, Ananias, was very angry at this speech, as it seemed as if Paul felt he was in the right. The wicked judge desired the men around to give Paul blows upon his mouth.

Then said Paul, 'God shall smite thee, thou whited wall!' He called him a whited wall; for the high priest was righteous outside when he sat to judge. People who stood near said to Paul, 'Why dost thou speak against the high priest?' Paul replied, 'I did not know he was the high priest; for it is written (in the Bible), Thou shalt not speak evil of the ruler.'*

* God did indeed smite this high-priest long afterwards, for he was forced to flee from his enemies into a hiding-place; and being found, he was cut to pieces by the soldiers who found him.

Paul was ready to own when he was in fault; for he was not, like Jesus, without sin.

The next thing that Paul said made his seventy judges quarrel together. Some of Paul's judges were Pharisees, and some were Sadducees. The Pharisees believed there would be a resurrection of the dead. The Sadducees believed scarcely anything they could not see.

So Paul cried out, 'I am a Pharisee, and the son of a Pharisee; and I am judged here because I hope that there will be a resurrection of the dead.' The Pharisees were pleased with Paul for saying this, but the Sadducees were angry; and they all began to speak so fiercely, that the captain feared they would soon fight, and tear Paul to pieces between them. Therefore he commanded the soldiers to take Paul away, and to bring him back to his prison in the castle.

It was much safer for Paul to be

IN THE CASTLE.

locked up there than to be left among the Jews. Yet any prison is very gloomy and mournful.

Paul spent another night in the castle, but it was a joyful night; for the Lord came and stood near him, and said, 'Be of good cheer, Paul; for as thou hast been my witness at Jerusalem, so thou shalt be my witness at Rome.'

Now Paul knew that his enemies would not be able to kill him, and that he would go to that great city, Rome—the grandest city in all the world, where Cæsar, the emperor of the world, reigned.

Paul had long wished to go to Rome, that he might speak for Jesus there, and turn many to the Lord. But he did not yet know *how* he was to get there.

'The God of all comfort, who comforteth us in all our tribulation.'—2 *Cor.* i. 4.

LII.

THE PLOT DISCOVERED.

Acts, xxiii. 12–22.

The next morning a young man went up the stairs leading to the castle. The place was well guarded by soldiers. The young man asked the centurion at the door whether he might see Paul. The centurion gave him leave.

Who was this young man? Was it Timothy? No; it was none of Paul's fellow-travellers, but it was a young man who loved him, and a young man well known at Jerusalem as a gentleman and a Christian.

When this young man entered Paul's prison-room he said, 'Uncle, I have something very important to tell you.' You see, this young man was Paul's nephew. He was his sister's son, but we do not know his name.

Paul wanted to know what he had

THE PLOT DISCOVERED.

to tell him so important. 'It is a dreadful plan that has been made by forty Jews to kill you, my uncle. These forty have made a vow, or promise, that they will not eat or drink till they have killed you. But how can they get at you? They have been to the chief priests, and have begged them to ask the captain to bring you down again to be judged by the Sanhedrim. Then they intend to hide themselves on the way, and suddenly to burst forth from their hiding-place, and to kill you on the spot.'

Paul thought that he ought to try to prevent this wickedness, though he well knew he should not be killed, for God had told him he should see Rome. He called a centurion who was close by, and said to him, 'Will you take this young man to the captain? for he has something to tell him.'

So the centurion brought him to the captain. The captain took the young man by the hand and led him into a room where he could be alone with him. 'Now,' said he, 'what have you to tell me?'

The young man told him all. He ended by saying, 'When the chief priests send to ask you to let Paul come down to the council, do not consent: for they are hoping that you will consent.' The captain answered, 'You may now go. Do not mention to any one that you have told me what the Jews intend to do.'

The young man readily promised this; for if the Jews had known that he had told the captain, they would surely have torn the nephew in pieces instead of the uncle.

This nephew had acted faithfully to his uncle, and had saved his life.

'Our soul is escaped as a bird out of the snare of the fowlers.'— *Ps.* cxxiv. 7.

LIII.

THE JOURNEY TO CÆSAREA.

Acts, xxiii. 23 to end.

The captain had a great deal to do before evening. His plan for saving Paul's life was to send him away secretly to another city.

There was a city called Cæsarea, thirty-five miles from Jerusalem. At that time the Roman governor was living there. The captain thought of sending Paul to be judged by that Roman governor; for that was a privilege that Paul enjoyed as a Roman citizen.

But if the Jews knew that Paul was going to leave the city they would attack Paul. Therefore the captain meant to send Paul by night, and to have him well guarded by soldiers.

The captain called two centurions, and said to them secretly, 'Get ready immediately two hundred soldiers.' Each centurion had a hundred under his command. 'But that will not be enough,' thought the captain. 'Get ready besides seventy horsemen and two hundred men, with spears and pikes. Be ready at nine o'clock,' said the captain. 'Take care that there are horses for Paul to ride on, and take him safe to the governor Felix at Cæsarea.'

Having given these orders the captain sat down to write a letter to the governor.

He began his letter thus: 'Claudius Lysias unto the most excellent governor Felix, sendeth greeting.'

He went on to say that Paul had done nothing deserving of death, or even of imprisonment, but that the Jews had accused him of disobeying their law.

He ended his letter nearly in these words: 'When it was told me that the Jews meant to lie in wait for the man,

I sent him to thee; and I commanded the Jews to go down to tell thee what he had done. Farewell.'

This letter the captain gave to the centurions to take to the governor.

At nine o'clock that evening, when it was dark, Paul mounted a horse, and a man chained to him rode on each side of Paul. Thus Paul left Jerusalem, accompanied by four hundred and seventy soldiers.

This was a little army, and this army was to guard one weak man. But that weak man had so many enemies that it was necessary to guard him well.

Softly and silently the little army departed from Jerusalem, and took the road to Cæsarea. During that night they went eighteen miles, and then they came to a town that lay on the way, where to rest. After resting during the day the four hundred foot-soldiers returned to Jerusalem, leaving only the seventy horsemen to guard Paul.

The next day Paul set out again on horseback, and in a few hours arrived at Cæsarea, by the sea-coast.

He was taken by a centurion to the governor's palace—a magnificent palace, built of white marble.

Paul was led into the grand room, where the governor, Felix, was sitting. This Felix was indeed a wicked old man. He was once a slave, but had been set free and made great. Why? Because he was ready to do any wicked thing that great men asked him to do. This old man was clothed in purple, and seated on a throne. Before him stood the holy prisoner, with chains on his hands.

The centurion presented the captain's letter to Felix. When the governor had read it, he asked where Paul came from. When he was told it was from Tarsus in Cilicia he looked towards Paul, and said, 'I will hear thee when thine accusers come down.'

Then he commanded him to be kept in the judgment-hall. He did not put him in a prison, but in a fine room close to the palace. In that room Paul slept that night.

'If any man suffer as a Christian, let him not be ashamed; but let him glorify God on this behalf.'—1 *Pet*. iv. 16.

LIV.

THE PRISON AT CÆSAREA.

Acts, xxiv. 1-23.

PAUL was again in Cæsarea. He had stayed there a little while ago in the house of Philip the deacon, with his four holy daughters; and he had seen Agabus the prophet. Did Paul now remember how Agabus had tied the girdle round his hands and feet, and shown that Paul would be chained in the same manner? O yes! Paul remembered it well; for it was only ten days ago since Agabus had done this.

Now Paul found himself with the real chains around his wrists and his ankles.

But though he was in chains, he was in a pleasant prison—for it was a fine, handsome, airy room—and kept cool by the sea-breezes.

He waited there three* days before his enemies arrived.

Ananias, the high priest, came, and the elders of the Sanhedrim.

There must have been a grand train of horses and servants, when such honourable men travelled

One morning Paul in his chains was called to appear before Felix, to be judged.

* In the text *five* days are mentioned, but they are counted from Paul's leaving Jerusalem, not from his arriving at Cæsarea.

THE PRISON AT CÆSAREA.

A whole host of enemies were assembled in the place. How full of malice they felt when they saw the poor prisoner, who had escaped out of their hands a few days before!

They had brought with them a man who could speak well: he was called an orator, or speaker. His name was Tertullus.

The Jews promised to pay him well for making a fine speech against Paul.

Tertullus began his speech by praising Felix. He continued it by abusing Paul. He pretended that Paul had gone about the world trying to make the Jews rebel; and that he had come to Jerusalem to profane the Temple.

When Tertullus had finished his speech, Felix made a sign for Paul to speak.

The prisoner declared he had done nothing wrong, and that no one could prove anything against him, except this one thing, that he had said,—

'There will be a resurrection of the dead!'

When Felix had heard Paul's answer, he did not know what to say. He thought that Paul was innocent. Why, then, did he not let him go? For the same reason that Pontius Pilate would not let Jesus go. He feared to displease the Jews. Still he was afraid to condemn a Roman citizen such as Paul. So he said to the Jews, 'I will wait till I know more of this matter; perhaps the captain may come down and tell me more.'

The Jews were very much disappointed by this answer; for they wanted to get Paul down to Jerusalem. But they were obliged to go home without him.

Felix liked Paul better than before, since he had heard his speech. He desired a centurion to take care of him, and to be kind to him, and to make him comfortable. He desired that Paul

THE PRISON AT CÆSAREA. 257

might be allowed to see his friends, and to have them stay with him.

This was a great delight to Paul. His friends were very dear to him. He might see Philip, who lived in Cæsarea. His daughters might come and bring him any food or clothes that he might want.

His friends at Jerusalem could easily come down and see him. Thirty-six miles is not a long journey. Perhaps the apostle James came down—perhaps Peter—perhaps John.

It is certain that Luke was often with Paul. Some think that he wrote his history of Jesus while sitting by Paul's side.

Timothy was sure to come; he was like a son to Paul, and was his greatest earthly comfort. There were many more who loved to be with the apostle. Would not Silas come and sing psalms with him, as he once did in a worse prison, a long while ago?

'Remember them that are in bonds, as bound with them; and them which suffer adversity, as being yourselves also in the body.'
—*Heb.* xiii. 3.

LV.

THE TREMBLING JUDGE.

Acts, xxiv. 24 to end.

Day after day passed away, and Paul continued in his pleasant prison.

Sometimes Felix went away for a while. Once he returned, bringing with him a beautiful young lady, whom he had just married.

Her name was Drusilla. She was a Jewess. She was the daughter of that Herod who put Peter in prison, and who was eaten by worms.

Yet, though a Jewess, she had just

married a heathen, and she had committed many crimes; for though so young, she had been married before, and she had left her husband to be the wife of Felix. The husband she had left was a king.*

It is reported that Simon Magus, whom Peter rebuked, had managed by his arts to set her against her right husband, and to turn her to like Felix.

When Felix brought Drusilla to Cæsarea, he told her of the wonderful prisoner he was keeping there. He told her how well Paul spoke about Jesus Christ, and His power to save those who believed in Him.

Felix thought that Drusilla would like to see this Jew, as she was a Jewess. So he desired the centurion to bring Paul out of prison into his room.

Paul was glad to speak of his Saviour to very great sinners. He knew that he stood before a wicked Gentile

* Azizus, king of the Emesenes.

governor, and a false, faithless Jewess. He spoke not only of Jesus as the Saviour, but also of Jesus as the Judge. He declared how terrible it would be for a sinner to stand before that Judge at the last day.

While the prisoner spoke of his Heavenly Judge, his earthly judge was seen to *tremble*. This was a good sign. It might be that he would not only tremble, but fall down and implore mercy, as Paul himself had once done. Oh, how he had trembled when he had said, 'Lord, what wilt Thou have me to do?'

But this aged sinner, Felix, when he trembled, commanded the preacher to depart.

'Go thy way for this time. When I have a convenient season I will call for thee.'

Paul was obliged to leave him, though he would gladly have stayed to persuade him to repent.

ACTS, XXIV. 25.

And as he reasoned of righteousness, temperance, and judgment to come, Felix trembled.'

THE TREMBLING JUDGE. 263

Felix often sent for Paul again and talked to him, but I do not hear that he ever trembled again. His heart was set upon getting money, and he sent so often for Paul, in hopes that Paul would offer him money to set him free. But Paul would not offer a bribe to a judge, even if he had the money, for it is wicked to offer bribes.

No doubt Paul's friends would have given him the money, if he had asked for it.

Felix went on in his covetousness for two years, and then another governor was sent by Cæsar at Rome to take his place.

Felix might have released Paul before he went away, but he thought it would please the Jews more if he left Paul in prison, and so he did. Thus he went on adding sin to sin, getting more and more hardened.

We do not know how *he* perished in this world, but we know that his wife

Drusilla, with her son, perished in an earthquake.

'The salvation of the righteous is of the Lord: He is their strength in the time of trouble. And the Lord shall help them, and deliver them; He shall deliver them from the wicked, and save them, because they trust in Him.'—*Ps.* xxxvii. 39, 40.

LVI.

THE DISAPPOINTMENT OF THE JEWS.

Acts, xxv. 1–12.

WHEN Felix went away, a new governor came in his place.

His name was Festus. He stayed only three days at Cæsarea, on his way to Jerusalem. During that short time he did not see Paul. But when he came to Jerusalem he heard a great deal about him. The chief priests and his friends came to Festus, and told him about a very bad man who lay in prison at Cæsarea.

'Oh, he has done so much harm!' they said. 'When he was free, he went from place to place setting people against Cæsar; he wants us all to rebel, and only to mind the laws of a man who once was crucified, Jesus of Nazareth, who, he says, is the true King.'

'What do you want me to do?' said Festus.

'We want you to send soldiers to fetch this wicked man, that you may judge him at Jerusalem. Do grant us this great favour, we entreat you —do let him come to Jerusalem.'

What made them so very anxious that Paul should go up to Jerusalem?

They wanted to hide themselves in

the road, and to burst forth upon him and kill him.

Those forty Jews, who lately made the same kind of plan, were among his accusers now, with Ananias at their head. Festus did not know the real motive of the Jews in wanting Paul to come to Jerusalem, but he did not grant their request, for he saw no use in bringing Paul back to Jerusalem.

Festus answered : 'I am going down to Cæsarea very soon, and when I go you can come with me, and you can accuse him before the judgment-seat *there* of all the wicked things you say he has done.

The Jews were much disappointed at this answer, but they were obliged to submit.

Festus stayed ten days at Jerusalem, and then he returned to Cæsarea. There went with him the chief priest and a troop of Paul's enemies.

The next day Festus sat on his

DISAPPOINTMENT OF THE JEWS. 267

judgment-seat in the palace, and the prisoner was brought forth to stand before him.

That prisoner saw once more his deadly enemies, who were panting for his blood. They had brought no great speaker with them this time, but they stood round about, pouring out of their spiteful lips loud and bitter complaints against Paul.

When Paul was allowed to speak, he said plainly,—'I have done nothing at all against any of them, nor against Cæsar. All I have done is to declare that Jesus, whom they crucified, is risen again from the dead.'

Festus saw that Paul had done nothing really wicked: but he was anxious to please the Jews, so he said to Paul,—'Will you go up to Jerusalem, and there be judged before me?'

This was just what the Jews wanted. They must have been pleased when they heard Festus say this.

'No,' said Paul : 'I will be judged before Cæsar.'

Paul was wise to refuse to go to Jerusalem. He chose to go to Rome instead, and God had told him (as you know) in a dream that he should go to Rome.

Festus could not refuse Paul's request, and he replied,—'As you wish to go to Cæsar, to Cæsar you shall go.'

Then Festus desired the centurion to take Paul back to his prison, and to keep him there, till he could send him in a ship to Rome.

The Jews went back to Jerusalem more disappointed than ever. They had lost their prey, they would never be able to stone him or to crucify him. He was to be taken far away.

'The Jews, who both killed the Lord Jesus, and their own prophets, and have persecuted us.'—1 *Thess.* ii. 15.

LVII.

KING AGRIPPA'S VISIT.

Acts, xxv. 13 to end; xxvi.

PAUL remained in prison while Festus, the governor, waited for a ship to carry the prisoner to Rome.

While Festus waited, a King came to see him. It was the son of that Herod who was eaten with worms.

His name was Herod Agrippa, but he is generally called Agrippa only.

He was a very great man—greater than Festus, for he was a king who could do what he would, while Festus was only a governor under Cæsar.

Agrippa brought with him his sister, Bernice.

Do you remember he had another sister, called Drusilla? but she was gone away with Felix. The whole family were very wicked.

As Agrippa was a Jew, he knew

more about the Jews' religion than Festus, who was a Roman.

Agrippa paid a very long visit to Festus.

One day Festus said to him, 'I should like you to see a man I have here in prison, named Paul. The Jews hate him very much, and yet I cannot find out that he has done anything wrong. They chiefly quarrel with him about one Jesus, whom the Jews say is dead, and who Paul says is alive. I would have taken him to Jerusalem to be judged, but he wishes to go to Rome, to be judged by Cæsar.'

Agrippa said he would like to hear the man speak.

'To-morrow,' said Festus, 'you shall hear him.'

The next day King Agrippa came into the great court, accompanied by the Princess Bernice, dressed in a very grand manner.

All the chief men came also.

Then Festus commanded that Paul should be brought forth. He came with his chains on his hands, a poor prisoner, mean and low in his appearance, but with Christ in his heart.

There were no accusers this time to speak first, so Agrippa commanded Paul to begin.

The prisoner stretched forth his chained hand, and spoke respectfully, saying, 'King Agrippa.' Then he told his history to the king, declaring how he had seen Jesus, as a light brighter than the sun, and how he had heard His voice.

'Therefore,' said he, 'I tell every one that Jesus died and rose again.'

When Festus heard him speak of rising from the dead, he cried out in a loud voice that Paul was mad.

Paul replied,—'I am not mad, most noble Festus! but speak forth the words of truth; and the king has heard about these things.'

Then Agrippa said, 'You almost persuade me to be a Christian.'

Paul gave him the most beautiful, loving answer,—'I would that you were not only *almost* but *altogether* such as I am, except these chains.' These were the chains upon his hands.

Then the king and the great people rose from their seats, and went into another room.

They said to one another, 'This man has done nothing to deserve death, or even chains.'

Agrippa said to Festus, 'If he had not asked to be judged by Cæsar, he might have been set free.'

But was Agrippa ever *quite* persuaded to be a Christian? No, never. He heard the truth, but he did not follow it at the moment he heard it.

He was not like the jailer at Philippi, who said, 'What must I do to be

ACTS, xxvi. 28.
'Then Agrippa said unto Paul, Almost thou persuadest me to be a Christian.'

T

saved?' and who believed that moment and was saved.

'And ye shall be brought before governors and kings for my sake.'—*Matt.* x. 18.

LVIII.

THE BEGINNING OF THE VOYAGE.

Acts, xxvii. 1–12.

At last a ship came to Cæsarea in which Paul could sail towards Rome. The ship was only going part of the way, but another ship might be found for the rest of the voyage.

Paul was given into the charge of a centurion named Julius. Was Paul to sail with none but strangers? Oh, no; he had two loving friends to accompany him—two friends who had travelled with him before, and who had probably been much with him in his prison. These were Aristarchus, a man of Macedonia, and Luke, the writer of Paul's history. What a comfort for Paul to have such friends, especially Luke, who knew so much about the Lord Jesus!

The people who sailed in the ship were the captain and his sailors, who worked the ship; the centurion and his soldiers, who guarded the prisoners; Paul, and his two friends. Besides Paul there were other prisoners, who may have committed great crimes. The prisoners were all to be judged at Rome.

The ship sailed along the coast of Cæsarea, till it came to Sidon, just above Cæsarea. Here the ship stopped. Paul had Christian friends in Sidon. He longed much to see them and to bid them farewell.

Julius, the centurion, was very kind to Paul, and he readily allowed him to go on shore and see his friends, and to get any comforts for the voyage that he needed. His friends would be sure to remember to give him some good food to take with him.

A cheering walk it was for Paul to go with Luke and Aristarchus to see those friends ; it was so long since he had paid a visit to any one : but there went with him a soldier, fastened to him by a chain, to see that he did not escape. The way was among hills, covered with fig-trees, orange-trees, and vineyards.

Paul returned to the ship and set sail again.

After going a long while by the shore of Asia, the ship met another that was going to Rome. The centurion made all on board get into the other ship.

And now the ship sailed very slowly for many days, for the wind was against it.

The ship sailed underneath the large island of Crete, and took shelter in a large harbour there, where it was sheltered from the high wind. This harbour was called 'The Fair Havens.'

The summer was now ended, and it was become rather dangerous to sail. The chief men on board consulted together about the voyage. 'Shall we stay here, or go on?'

'This is a good haven where we are,' said one; 'shall we pass the winter here?'

'Oh, no,' said another; 'there is a much better haven a little further on.'

'Let us try to reach it,' said another.

Then Paul, though a prisoner, gave his advice. He said, 'Sirs, I perceive that in this voyage there will be danger to the goods in the ship, and to the ship itself, and to our lives.'

But the centurion would not follow his advice, for he thought that the captain and the owner of the ship knew better than Paul. Most of the sailors and soldiers on board wished to go on. 'Surely we can go forty miles more to the good port!' said they.

Ah! they knew not that Paul was a prophet, and that he would not have given his advice, except by the will of God.

Just at this time the wind blew very softly. The crew set sail, and they went along so pleasantly that they must have been glad that they did not follow Paul's advice. In a few hours they hoped to reach the well-sheltered haven, at the further end of the island of Crete.

'If any man lack wisdom, let him ask of God, that giveth to all men liberally.'—*Jam.* i. 5.

LIX.

THE STORM AT SEA.
Acts, xxvii. 13-26.

The soft south wind was soon changed for a very high and terrible north-east wind.

And now the ship was tossed up and down, like a mad thing.

In all haste the sailors got her under the shelter of a little island (named Clauda), and then tried to get up the boat, which floated after them tied by a rope. It was hard work to get this boat on board When they had got it up, they wound the rope round the ship to keep it together, for they were afraid the boards would split and the ship go to pieces. What straining of arms! what pulling! what dragging! were seen that day on deck, as the wretched crew bound the ropes around their battered vessel!

The tossing of the waves continued

till the sailors thought they must make the ship lighter, by casting away all heavy things; so beds and boards, chains and poles, were thrown into the sea.

But the ship seemed nothing the better for it all, as the wind was as furious as ever.

And now the men on board began to give up all hope of being saved. But Paul knew that he himself could not be lost, because God had declared to him long ago that he should see Rome. But this was not enough for Paul; his loving heart desired that *all* in the ship might be saved, and he made continual prayer to God for every one.

And God answered him by sending an angel in the night to comfort him.

For some time past the sun had never been seen in the sky, through the dark clouds overhead; nor had the moon or stars appeared.

No one could sit down to take a meal,—all were too wretched and too ill. Even Paul did not eat, for his heart was full of care for the rest.

One day he stood up on deck in the midst of the trembling troop of sailors and soldiers, and spoke. Midst the howling of the winds and roaring of waves he spoke, and all *now* listened to every word,—' Sirs, you should have listened to me, and not have left that haven in Crete. But now, be of good cheer; there shall be no loss of any man's life among you, but only of the ship; for there stood by me this night the angel of God (whose I am and whom I serve), and said, " Fear not, Paul; thou must be brought before Cæsar; and lo, God hath given thee all those who sail with thee." So, sirs, be of good cheer, for I believe God, that it shall be as it was told me, only we must be shipwrecked upon an island.'

Paul knew not the name of that island.

All the ship's company now saw

that Paul was a prophet. We may be sure that he told them of Jesus, who died for them and rose again; for Paul never forgot he was God's servant, as he said, 'Whose I am, and whom I serve.'

'They mount up to the heaven, they go down again to the depths.' —*Ps.* cvii. 26.

LX.

THE LAST NIGHT OF THE VOYAGE.

Acts, xxvii. 27–38.

Day after day the ship continued to be tossed about by the waves.

Fourteen days had now passed away since the ship had left the Fair Havens in Crete. All this time it had been rolling upon the moving ocean, the crew not knowing when it would reach land.

The sailors often let down the plummet to measure the depth of the ocean. This plummet was a rope with a stone or some weight at the end. The sailors knew that if land was near, the sea would be less deep.

One night when the plummet was let down, the sailors found that the sea was not very deep. When let down again, they found the sea was still less deep.

They now hoped that land was near. They were glad, yet they were frightened, for there are often rocks near the shore. They dreaded lest the ship should be dashed against rocks and broken to pieces. So they thought it best to make it stop its course. They let down four anchors to hook it fast to the bottom of the sea; for one anchor would not have been strong enough in such a rough sea.

After this was done the people in the ship longed very earnestly for the sun to rise.

The sailors did very wrong this night. They made a plan of escaping in the little boat. Yet they knew that the other people in the ship could not do without them, as none but sailors can manage a ship.

Though it was dark, Paul knew what those selfish sailors were going to do, and he told the centurion. He said to him and to the soldiers, 'Except those sailors stay in the ship, you (soldiers) cannot be saved.'

Then the soldiers cut the ropes that fastened the boat to the ship, and soon the boat was tossed to a distance.

Now the sailors *could* not get in it.

The darkness was not yet gone. All on board were watching for the light with anxious hearts, and the light was beginning to come.

Then Paul spoke to them all. He said they had now been fourteen days without eating a *meal*, and that they needed food. No doubt every one had taken a morsel now and then, but not a meal.

Then Paul begged them to eat. 'For,' said he, 'there shall not an hair fall from the head of any of you.'

It was his God who told him this.

Then Paul took some bread, and gave thanks to God in the presence of all on board.

The heathen men heard Paul give thanks to the God of Heaven, the Father of the Lord Jesus Christ. Who can tell but that some believed and were saved?

After grace Paul broke the bread, and began to eat.

Then all on board felt cheerful and happy, and they also ate bread.

There was a great number to eat bread—two hundred and seventy-six—and many loaves must have been eaten in that night-breakfast.

Afterwards they were strong enough

to throw some more things into the sea, especially a quantity of wheat.

They were in hopes of keeping the ship from sinking, but Paul had told them some time ago that it must be lost.

Oh, how they longed to know where they were!

But it was now November, near winter, and the sun did not rise till half-past six.

'Their soul is melted because of trouble.'—*Ps.* cvii. 26.

LXI.

THE SHIPWRECK.

Acts, xxvii. 39 to end.

AT last the day dawned. The ship's company looked up and saw land at a short distance.

The shore was rocky and dangerous. In the midst of it was an opening, called a creek. At the entrance to the creek a heap of mud and clay was concealed.

The sailors tried to drive the ship into this creek. First, they lifted up the anchors, to set the ship free, and then they unfurled the chief sail to get forward.

They did not know there was a mass of clay and mud under the water,* till the ship stuck fast in it, and so they could get no further.

Very soon the violence of the waves broke the hinder part of the ship, and quite destroyed it.

The soldiers then made a very wicked proposal.

They said to the centurion, 'Is there not a risk of the prisoners escaping into the sea, and running away? Will not the judges of Rome be very angry?

* Alford.

Had we not better kill the prisoners? For if we tell the judges at Rome that we killed them, they will not punish us, but they will if we say the prisoners got away.'

This plan was very selfish and cruel. Shall Paul be killed?

There were other prisoners besides Paul. They may have been wicked men, but still they ought not to be killed before they were tried.

The centurion did not agree to the soldiers' plan, for he loved Paul and wished to save him. Well he might, for had not Paul saved all their lives? For it was he who hindered the sailors from getting off in the boat, as they meant slily to do.

'No,' answered the centurion to the ungrateful soldiers: 'none of the prisoners shall be killed. Let them swim to land if they can.'

So they did swim to land. I believe Paul could swim, for he had once—a long while ago—been a night and a day in the deep.

Those who could not swim caught hold of boards and broken pieces of the ship, and got safe to land.

Not one of the two hundred and seventy-six was lost in the wreck. No, not a hair of their heads was hurt.

They were wet and cold, but they had not a limb bruised or a bone broken. Only the ship was lost.

Thus all that Paul said came true. Perhaps Julius, the kind centurion, may now have believed, but the deceitful sailors and the cruel soldiers had not believed.

'All thy waves and thy billows are gone over me.'—*Ps.* xlii. 7.

LXII.

THE VIPER

Acts, xxviii. 1–6.

When all the shipwrecked men came to land they saw people on the shore. They found that the place was an island, called Melita. (Its name now is Malta.)

The inhabitants were rather wild. They were neither Greeks nor Romans, so they were called barbarians by those proud nations. They were ignorant of books, and they wore rough clothes, but they were kind-hearted. When they saw the poor, shivering, dripping strangers on the shore, they quickly lighted a large fire, and gave to all whatever they needed. It was now raining, and the poor creatures must have wanted dry clothes.

Paul, instead of warming himself by the fire, went about gathering sticks to keep it up. He did not think that a great apostle ought not to help, but let others gather sticks. No; he was ready to do anything—he was so humble. He brought a bundle of sticks and laid it on the fire,—when suddenly out of the flame sprang a viper, and lo, it fastened on Paul's hand!

That viper had been coiled around some sticks that Paul had gathered, and perhaps it was then asleep, or half frozen; but the heat had revived it, and made it spring out of the fire. There it was—with its fangs in the apostle's flesh, hanging down from his hand.

The barbarians looked at it, and knew it to be a viper, whose bite would kill. They said to each other, 'No doubt that man is a murderer, who has escaped drowning in the sea; but justice will not allow him to live. They thought that their gods were angry with him, and were going to punish him.

Acts, xxviii. 5.
'And he shook off the beast into the fire, and felt no harm.'

But Paul shook off the viper from his hand into the fire, and he felt no harm at all from the bite.

The barbarians kept on looking at Paul, expecting to see him swell and fall down dead suddenly; but they looked a great while and saw no harm come to him. Then they changed their minds, and said that he was a god.

We are sure that Paul would not let them worship him. You remember how he forbade the men at Lystra to worship him and Barnabas; and he had the same feelings still. He desired nothing, but to bring the barbarians to worship the true God, the Father of the Lord Jesus Christ. The best reward he could give them for all their kindness was to tell them of the Saviour.

'These signs shall follow them that believe; they shall take up serpents.'—*Mark*, xvi. 18.

LXIII.

LANDING IN ITALY.

Acts, xxviii. 7-15.

A VERY rich man lived close by the place where Paul was shipwrecked. His name was Publius. We believe he was the governor of the island. This island belonged to the Romans, and had a governor from Rome.

But though Publius was a Roman and a heathen, he was very kind to the apostle, and invited him and his friends to stay three days in his house.

What a change it was for Paul, after being so long in prison, to come to a fine house, and to be treated with honour! Luke and Aristarchus, of course, came with him, and probably Julius, the kind centurion. It is certain that he praised Paul, and that he told Publius that he did not deserve to be a prisoner.

It was a good thing for Publius that he invited Paul to his house, for the poor old father of Publius lived there, and he now lay ill of a very bad fever. When Paul heard of it he went into the old man's room and prayed, and laid his hands on him and healed him.

The news of this miracle soon spread wide, and a number of sick people flocked around Paul to be healed;—and they were healed.

When Paul left the house of Publius there were many doors open to him. Every one wanted to have such a wonderful man in his house.

Paul stayed in the island three months. During all that time he preached and prayed, and he showed many poor barbarians the way of salvation.

At the end of three months the spring was come, and the sea was smooth. The centurion hired a ship to take his whole company to the shores of Rome.

Paul now parted from his new friends in Malta. He found them very grateful. They loaded Paul and his friends, Luke and Aristarchus, with many presents.

Paul and his friends were much in need of clothing, for they had lost all at sea. But everything they wanted, whether clothing or nice food, was supplied to them.

There are many dried fruits, such as figs and raisins, in hot countries; and there is abundance of oranges. Everything refreshing was put into the ship by the generous barbarians. We may be sure that a blessing rested upon them for all this kindness to God's people.

The ship sailed with a fair wind to the shores of Italy, till it came to a fine harbour called Pu-te-o-li, more than a hundred miles from Rome.

This harbour was a grand place. Ships from all parts rode on its smooth waters. The shore was beautiful, for its hills were planted with gardens. Here Paul landed, still chained to a soldier, accompanied by his friends. Great was his joy to find Christians ready to receive him. The kind Julius allowed him to spend seven days with his friends.

The day came for the centurion to lead his prisoner to Rome. He took him along a well-paved road, very near the sea-coast. Every twenty miles there was a kind of inn for the travellers to rest.

On the road Paul met some friends, who had come from Rome on purpose to welcome him. Seeing them pleased his heart so much that he thanked God and took courage.

At last he arrived at Rome, with a troop of loving friends around him, as well as the soldier to whom he was chained.

'Beloved, let us love one another: for love is of God; and

every one that loveth is born of God, and knoweth God.'—1 *John*, iv. 7.

LXIV.

ARRIVAL AT ROME.

Acts, xxviii. 16 to end.

When Paul was arrived in Rome, where did he go? As he was a prisoner, he ought to have been taken to the place where the soldiers lived. It was a great square with buildings on every side, and a great ditch outside. But he was not taken to that noisy, crowded place, like the other prisoners.

Paul was allowed to live in a lodging of his own, though he was always to be chained to a soldier.

Do you ask why he was allowed this great privilege of living in a lodging? I suppose it was through the kindness of Julius, the centurion.

ARRIVAL AT ROME. 301

The Lord will not forget this kindness of Julius, if it was done because he loved Jesus.

Do you ask how it was that Paul could pay for a lodging? I suppose it was through the kindness of his friends in Rome. There were a great many in Rome who loved Paul much.

When Paul had stayed three days in Rome, he sent a message to the chief Jews in the city. The message was—to ask them to come to see him in his lodging.

The chief Jews were soon on the way to see Paul. They had often heard of him, but very few had ever seen him; and they must have longed to see such a wonderful man.

They found him weak and worn, bowed down with age and sorrow, but full of love and kindness. The soldier was chained to his arm.

Paul thought these Jews might have heard from other Jews that he had done something wicked.

ARRIVAL AT ROME.

Paul assured them that he had done nothing to deserve being in chains. All he had done to offend the Jews was to preach about the resurrection.

The Jews told Paul that they should like to know what he preached about.

Then Paul fixed a day for them to come again to hear him.

Early in the morning they came. Paul then began to explain to them out of the prophets all about Jesus. He showed them how Isaiah called Him a lamb brought to the slaughter; how David said His hands and feet should be pierced, and many other such things.

All day long Paul spoke about Jesus. When the evening came the Jews talked together.

One said: 'Paul speaks the truth. I believe that Jesus died and rose again.'

Another Jew said: 'But I do not believe what Paul says.'

ACTS, xxviii. 23.

'And when they had appointed him a day, there came many to him into his lodging; to whom he expounded and testified the kingdom of God.'

In this way they disputed together.

Before they went away, Paul told the unbelieving Jews that the Gentiles would hear of the Saviour, and would believe in Him.

The Jews went home, talking all the way about what Paul had said.

For two whole years Paul dwelt in his own lodging. Any one, who wished to be taught, might come to him.

Though Paul could not preach in the synagogues, or in the streets, or on the hills, he could preach in his house. No one forbade him to preach, and many people came to him.

This is the last thing said of him in the Acts. Perhaps Luke wrote his history at this time, for it ends here.

'Some believed the things which were spoken, and some believed not.'—*Acts,* xxviii. 24.

LXV.

PAUL'S FRIENDS AND VISITORS AT ROME.

We know from other books a little more about Paul. Though he was chained to a soldier, he was able in his lodging to see his friends. He calls two of them his fellow-prisoners, Aristarchus of Macedonia, and Epaphras of Colosse. He had visits from Mark, Justus, Demas, and Luke. Timothy was a great comfort to him, and was as dear to him as if he had been his own son.

He was able also to preach to all who liked to come and hear him. Amongst them came a slave whose name was Onesimus. He had run away from a very pious master; and he had not only run away, but had also robbed him. The master's name was Philemon. When Onesimus heard Paul preach, he repented, and confessed all to him. He was full of sorrow for his sin, and of love to the Apostle. He could now have been a great comfort to the poor prisoner. But instead of keeping him, Paul sent him back to his master at Colosse with a letter. In this letter, Paul speaks to Philemon of his chains and of his prison; he tells him how Onesimus had been converted by his preaching, just as Philemon himself once had been; he offers to pay back all that had been stolen, and he entreats him to give Onesimus his liberty. He seems to wish to have him back again. He ends his letter by saying he hopes soon to be free himself, and then to go and see Philemon and his dear wife Apphia, and their son Archippus, who was a minister at Colosse. We do not know what answer Philemon sent to this epistle, but we feel sure that he granted the request.

Another of Paul's friends was Tychicus, who had been one of his companions on his journey from Macedonia to Jerusalem. Some people think that Tychicus now came to Rome with tidings of the Ephesians, and that Paul in return sent him back to them.

Paul was very anxious they should know how he fared in prison, and he gave Tychicus a beautiful letter to give them. It was full of tender love and holy advice. No one was forgotten in it. Masters, servants, husbands, wives, parents, even the children, were remembered—they were specially encouraged to be obedient, in order to show their love to the Lord Jesus.

Paul's heart was so full of love that he wrote another letter besides, and gave it to Tychicus and Onesimus to take for him. This letter was to the Colossians, whom he had never seen. He had heard of them from their minister Epaphras.

After Paul had been in prison some

time, he was much comforted by a visit from one of his greatest friends, a very good man indeed. You have not heard of him before. His name was Epaphroditus, and he came from Philippi. Of all Paul's friends, none loved him more than the Philippians. They now showed their tender love by sending him a present, just such a present as would be most useful to an aged prisoner. They sent it without having been asked for it, because they loved the Apostle so dearly that they longed to do something to comfort him.

We may be sure that Epaphroditus was pleased to bring the present. Perhaps in his haste to reach the Apostle he travelled too quickly, for he fell very ill, and almost died. How earnestly Paul prayed God to restore him, and to spare him the great affliction of losing this dear friend! The Lord heard this prayer, and restored him. Epaphroditus hoped that the

Philippians would not hear of his illness, lest they should be unhappy and anxious.* He was much distressed to learn that they knew of it. Paul wrote them a long letter. He told them he knew how much they loved him, and he told them he was no longer in the lodging. As his trial was soon to take place, he was removed to the barracks of the soldiers. He told them how God had comforted him in his imprisonment by converting some of the servants of the wicked Emperor Nero. Now he did not know whether he should be set free or put to death. If the Lord had given him his choice, he would not have known what to choose. He liked nothing so much as the thought of dying and being with Jesus; but then he liked also to live, in order to preach about Christ. He knew the Philippians prayed God to spare his life, and he thought God would grant their prayers.

* Philip. ii. 26.

He thanked them very much for their presents, which showed their tender love to him; and he felt sure God would reward them for it, as he asked Him.

Epaphroditus took this letter back to them. Great must have been their joy at seeing the good minister return well, after his long journeys and dangerous illness! No doubt it encouraged them to pray that the beloved Apostle himself might soon be restored to them.

At last the trial came. He was brought before the cruel Emperor Nero. The prayers of God's people were granted. Paul was set at liberty. We believe he went to see his old friends. He went to Ephesus, and made Timothy bishop there. He took Titus to Crete, and set him over the churches there. Afterwards he went to Macedonia, and when he was there he wrote to Timothy and Titus. In these letters he tells them how ministers should behave, and how they ought to teach.

Paul loved to go and preach to the heathen, who had never heard the Gospel. Some people think that he went to Spain, as he had long meant to do.

His plan was to spend the winter at Nicopolis, and he desired Titus to come to him there, and bring Tychicus, Zenas, and Apollos. We do not know whether he did meet them there. It seems that about this time he was again made prisoner, and carried to Rome. The second time he was brought there as a prisoner, he was not treated as well as he had been before. We do not read of his having a lodging of his own. Except Luke, none of his old friends stood by him. All forsook him and fled, but Demas behaved the worst. He loved the present world better than Christ. In his heart the good seed was choked by the thorns and thistles. Paul was left alone.

Yet one good man loved him so much as to seek him out. This good man was called Onesiphorus. Everywhere he searched for Paul, till he found him in prison, and helped and comforted him. Paul's cruel enemies now came forward and accused him, and did him all the harm they could; one in particular, a coppersmith named Alexander.* Soon Paul was brought before the judgment. No one helped him. No one stood by him. Yet the Lord was with him.

Paul was sent back to prison. This prison is supposed to have been the Mamertine Prison, which had only two rooms. Both were underground, but one was lower than the other. They

* Some people think that this was the very Jew who had opposed Paul at Ephesus (Acts, xix. 33), and that he had now been sent to Rome on purpose to injure him. (See Lewin's *Life of St. Paul,* vol. ii. p. 391.) Others think, that when Paul put Timothy on his guard against Alexander, he was speaking only of his conduct at Ephesus, and not of anything he had done at Rome.

had no windows. All the light and air they ever had, came through a hole in the roof and in the floor of the upper room. They had no doors: all who entered them had to go through the hole. They had no fresh air and no drainage, yet the upper room was sometimes filled with prisoners. Some were fastened to iron rings fixed in the stone walls. Some were stretched on the cold, damp floor, with their feet in the stocks.

The only pleasure the poor prisoners ever had was to see those kind friends who were brave enough to visit them.

From his prison Paul wrote to Timothy, and begged him to come to him as soon as possible, and bring his cloak with him, as he felt the cold very much. Paul may have left this cloak at Troas long before, when he had walked to Assos. He was very poor, and he could not afford to lose it. He told Timothy he felt his end was near. He was not afraid of death. He knew there was a glorious crown waiting for him, and for all who loved the Lord. He felt sure that he should never write to Timothy again, and so he gave him a great deal of good advice.

Did Paul see Timothy at Rome? We do not know. But we know the Apostle was soon brought again to trial, and condemned to have his head cut off. How Timothy must have mourned if he arrived too late, and heard only of his death!

Yet he wished to die for Jesus, and he had his wish.

When the Lord returns in glory Paul will come with Him, no longer poor, aged, worn, but beautiful and glorious, to reign with Him, for it is written,—

'They that turn many to righteousness (shall shine) as the stars, for ever and ever.'—*Dan.* xii. 3.

LXVI.

THE GLORIOUS VISIONS OF JOHN.

The whole Book of the Revelation.

W<small>E</small> read nothing more in the Bible about any of the apostles, except John.

The last book in the Bible gives an account of the wonderful things he saw in his old age.

After Nero Cæsar was dead, another wicked Cæsar reigned, named Domitian. He sent John to a little rocky island near Greece. It was named Patmos, and there wicked men, who had committed great crimes, were often sent to work hard at digging up stones.

The island is only a quarter the size of Malta. Any one could walk round it in a day. It is full of mountains. There are caves among the mountains.

THE VISIONS OF JOHN. 317

In this rugged island John was made to live But on the Lord's day he heard a voice behind him as of a trumpet, and looking back he saw his Saviour, the Lord Jesus. He wore now a glorious body, quite different from that suffering body on which John once leaned his head. Now John was so filled with fear that he fell at His feet as dead. Then Jesus laid His hand upon him and said,—

'I am He that liveth and was dead, and behold, I am alive for evermore.' Then He told John to write seven letters to Christians who lived in seven places in Asia.

The first letter was to Ephesus, where Paul had preached, and where John had lived a long while.

It was a short letter, praising the Christians for some things, and blaming them for not loving Jesus as much as they once did.

After John had written the seven

letters in the words of Jesus, he looked and saw a door opened in heaven, and he heard a voice saying, 'Come up hither, and I will show thee things which shall happen hereafter.'

So John was in the Spirit, and saw a throne in Heaven, and One shining on the throne; a rainbow round about the throne; and a Lamb as it had been slain in the midst of the throne; and many glorious saints and angels round the throne, singing the praises of the Father and the Son.

They praised the Father—because He created all things; and they praised the Lamb—because He had redeemed His people by His blood.

John saw many terrible sights.

He saw hail, and fire, and blood, and smoke, and brimstone, and plagues, and devils, and earthquakes.

At last he saw Jesus come with His saints to punish the wicked. He came like a great warrior, on a white horse;

followed by armies on white horses, clothed in linen white and clean.

He saw the old serpent shut up in a pit, so deep that it had no bottom, for a thousand years.

He saw the righteous dead reign with Christ for a thousand years.

He saw Satan let loose for a little while, and in the end he saw him cast into the lake of fire and brimstone, to be tormented for ever and ever.

He saw the great white throne, and all men stand before God to be judged. He saw the dead rise from their graves, and he saw some cast into the lake of fire.

He saw a city come down from heaven to the earth, shining like precious stones. He heard that all whose names were written in the Lamb's book of life shall live in this city.

An angel showed him all these things, and told him about them.

But Jesus spoke to him also and

said, 'All liars shall have their part in the lake which burneth with fire and brimstone.'

Jesus ended by saying, 'Surely I come quickly.'

And John answered, 'Even so; come, Lord Jesus.'

'Behold, he cometh with clouds; and every eye shall see him, and they also which pierced him: and all kindreds of the earth shall wail because of him.'—*Rev.* i. 7.

QUESTIONS TO BE ASKED AFTER READING EACH CHAPTER.

I.

1. Who wrote the Acts?
2. Was Luke one of the twelve apostles?
3. What else did he write besides the Acts?
4. What promise did the angels make when Jesus ascended?
5. From what mountain did He ascend?
6. Why did they wait at Jerusalem?
7. What did they do in the upper room?
8. Who first stood up to preach?
9. What did he propose their doing?
10. How did they know whom God had chosen'
11. What was his name?

II.

1. How long after Christ's ascension did the Holy Ghost come down?
2. How long after His resurrection?
3. At what feast of the Jews?
4. Why was it called Pentecost?
5. In what manner did the Holy Ghost descend?

6. What wonder did He enable those to do who received Him?
7. Did they remain in the upper room?
8. Who preached to the multitude?
9. How many were baptized afterwards?

III.

1. Whom did Peter and John heal at the Temple gate?
2. Who preached again?
3. What did he say in his sermon?

IV.

1. Where did Peter and John spend that night?
2. Who were their judges next morning?
3. Why did they not punish them again?
4. What command did they give the apostles?
5. What brave answer did the apostles give?

V.

1. What generous action did Barnabas do?
2. Who wanted to appear as good as he was?
3. How did he try to deceive Peter?
4. What did Peter say to Ananias?
5. What happened to Ananias?
6. What questions did Peter ask Sapphira?
7. What befell Sapphira?

VI.

1. What did people feel who heard of these judgments?
2. What did the high priest and his friends do to the apostles when they heard of their miracles?
3. Who released them in the night?
4. When the judges sent for them, where were they found?
5. How did they punish them?
6. Did they let them go?

VII.

1. What did the widows dispute about?
2. How did the apostles stop their murmuring?
3. Tell me the names of two of the deacons?

VIII.

1. Who was Stephen?
2. Before what judges was he brought?
3. Of what sin did he accuse them?
4. How did they kill him?
5. Who took care of their clothes?
6. What were Stephen's dying prayers?
7. What is Stephen called because he died for Christ's sake?

IX.

1. Who would not leave Jerusalem?
2. Where did Philip the deacon preach?
3. What wicked man pretended to turn to Jesus?

X.

1. Why did Peter and John go to Samaria?
2. Why did Simon offer them money?
3. What did Peter say to him?

XI.

1. Where did God send Philip?
2. Whom did he see there?
3. What was the rich man doing?
4. What could he not understand?
5. What did Philip do to him?
6. Where did Philip go?
7. Where did the rich man go?

XII.

1. To what city did Saul go?
2. What did he see on the way?
3. What did he hear?
4. What did he answer?
5. Why was he led by the hand?
6. How long did he sit still?

XIII.

1. What dream comforted Saul?
2. What dream did Ananias have?
3. What did he say to Saul?
4. What did Saul do in Damascus?

XIV.

1. Into what desert did Saul go?
2. Why did he return to Damascus?
3. Who tried to kill him?
4. Who helped them?
5. How did he escape?
6. Where did he go?

XV.

1. Whom did Saul wish to see in Jerusalem?
2. Why were the disciples afraid of him?
3. Who was very kind to him?

XVI.

1. What four men were great friends in Jerusalem?
2. Why did Saul leave Jerusalem?
3. Where did he go in a ship?

XVII.

1. What man with the palsy did Peter heal?
2. What woman did he raise?
3. Who were weeping for her?
4. Where did Tabitha live?
5. Where did Peter lodge?

XVIII.

1. What strange sight did Peter see in a dream?
2. What strange command did God give him?
3. Who sent to ask Peter to come?
4. Why had the dream been sent to Peter?

XIX.

1. Whom did Peter take with him to Cornelius?
2. To what place did he go?
3. What did Peter forbid Cornelius to do?
4. Why had Cornelius sent for Peter?
5. How did Peter know that Cornelius ought to be baptized?

XX.

1. Which of the apostles was killed first?
2. Whom did Herod mean to kill next?
3. What happened to Peter the night before he was to be killed?
4. To whose house did he go?

XXI.

1. What became of the soldiers who guarded Peter?
2. In what town did Herod make a fine speech?
3. What did the people say who heard him?
4. How did God punish Herod?

XXII.

1. Who fetched Saul from Tarsus?
2. Where did he take him?
3. What for?

XXIII.

1. Who went with Saul on his first missionary journey?
2. To what island did they go?
3. Who was Sergius Paulus?
4. Who tried to prevent him from believing?
5. How did Saul punish him?

XXIV.

1. What change was made in Saul's name?
2. Where was Perga?
3. Who left the apostles at that place?
4. At Antioch, in Pisidia, who were angry at Paul's preaching?
5. To whom did Paul turn?

XXV.

1. Why did the apostles leave Iconium secretly?
2. What miracle did Paul work at Lystra?
3. How were the people going to honour them?
4. What did they do to Paul at last?

XXVI.

1. Why did Paul visit those cities again where he had been so ill-used?
2. To what city did he return when his journey was ended?
3. What did some Jews say that caused trouble to the believers?
4. Why did Paul go to Jerusalem?
5. What did the apostles write in the letter they sent back to Antioch in Syria?

XXVII.

1. Why did not Saul go with Barnabas on his second missionary journey?
2. Whom did Paul take?
3. Whom did he find at Lystra and take with him?

XXVIII.

1. What dream did Paul have at Troas?
2. What third companion had Paul now got?
3. To what city in Macedonia did they first go?
4. What woman believed?

XXIX.

1. How did Paul make some covetous men at Philippi very angry ?
2. What did the judges order to be done to Paul and Silas ?
3. How did the jailer treat them ?

XXX.

1. What sound was heard in the dungeon ?
2. What shook the dungeon ?
3. Who was much afraid ?
4. What was he going to do ?
5. What question did he ask Paul and Silas ?
6. What did they reply ?
7. How did the jailer show he was changed ?

XXXI.

1. What message did the judges send the next morning ?
2. Why did Paul refuse to go ?
3. What did the judges beg them to do ?
4. To whose house did the apostles go ?

XXXII.

1. When they left Philippi, to what great city by the sea did the apostles go ?
2. Who was Jason ?

3. Why did Jason hide Paul and Silas?
4. Why did they go away in the night?

XXXIII.

1. To what quiet town did they go?
2. How did the Bereans find that all Paul said was true?
3. From what place did wicked Jews come?
4. To what place did the Bereans take Paul?

XXXIV.

1. Where was Athens?
2. How did the Athenians spend their time?
3. Why did they take Paul to Mars' Hill?
4. What did they laugh at?

XXXV.

1. What were the chief pleasures at Corinth?
2. With whom did Paul lodge?
3. Why?
4. What friends came to Paul at Corinth?
5. What did he do in the evening besides weaving goats' hair?
6. From what place did Paul's friends bring him presents?

XXXVI.

1. Why did Paul leave off going to the synagogue at Corinth?
2. In whose house did he preach?
3. How did God comfort him?
4. What sort of a judge was Gallio?
5. Who sailed in a ship from Corinth?
6. Why did Paul land at Cenchrea?
7. What good woman was there?
8. Where did he leave Priscilla and Aquila?
9. What did Paul promise the Ephesians?
10. To what city did Paul return at the end of his second journey?

XXXVII.

1. After Paul was gone, what new preacher came to Ephesus?
2. What was it he did not know?
3. Who instructed him?
4. Why did he take letters into Greece?

XXXVIII.

1. Who was Paul's companion on his *third* missionary journey?
2. To what provinces in Asia did he go?
3. To what great city did he go as he had promised?

XXXIX.

1. Did he find Apollos at Ephesus?
2. What twelve men did he find there?
3. Where did Paul preach when he could not go to the synagogue?
4. What miracles did he work?

XL.

1. What great preacher came to Ephesus while Paul was there?
2. What sad news did he bring?
3. Why did Paul pay a short visit to Corinth?
4. Whom did he send there?
5. Whom did he send with the letter he wrote?
6. How did the Corinthians receive Paul's letter?

XLI.

1. For what wickedness was Ephesus famous?
2. Who was Sceva?
3. How were his sons treated by an evil spirit?
4. How did other sorcerers show their repentance?

XLII.

1. In whose honour was the temple at Ephesus built?
2. What did Demetrius make and sell?

3. Who stirred up the other silversmiths?
4. What did they all cry out?
5. How was the uproar quieted?

XLIII.

1. To what city did Paul go on leaving Ephesus?
2. Who came there that Paul had been longing to see?
3. What news did he bring which rejoiced Paul?
4. What request did Paul make to all countries?

XLIV.

1. When Paul preached at Troas, who fell out of the window?
2. How did Paul comfort those who mourned for the youth?
3. How many companions had Paul now with him?

XLV.

1. Did Paul go in a ship from Troas?
2. Where did he get in?
3. Why did not Paul stop at Ephesus?
4. Where did he stop?
5. Whom did he send for?
6. What did he say which grieved them most?

XLVI.

1. What did the Christians of Tyre tell Paul?
2. Where did they part?
3. Whom did Paul visit at Cæsarea?
4. What did Agabus do with Paul's girdle?
5. What did they all entreat?
6. What did they say at last?

XLVII.

1. When Paul came to Jerusalem, where did he lodge?
2. What rejoiced all the brethren?

XLVIII.

1. What advice did some of the elders at Jerusalem give to Paul?
2. How did some Jews from Asia set the people against Paul?
3. Who stopped them from beating Paul?

XLIX.

1. From what place did Paul speak to the people?
2. What did Paul say that enraged them still more?

L.

1. What did the captain desire a centurion to do to Paul?
2. How did Paul prevent the soldiers scourging him?
3. Where did Paul sleep that night?

LI.

1. Where was Paul taken in the morning?
2. What did Paul say to the high priest which made him angry?
3. What did the judges quarrel about?
4. What did God say to Paul the next night?

LII.

1. What young man asked to see Paul in the castle?
2. What plot did he tell him of?
3. To whom did he send the young man?
4. What did the young man ask the captain not to do?

LIII.

1. What was the captain's plan for saving Paul?
2. Whom did he send with Paul to guard him?
3. To whom did he write a letter?

4. How did Paul ride?
5. Where was Paul taken?
6. Who was the governor?
7. Where did Paul sleep?

LIV.

1. Who came from Jerusalem to accuse Paul?
2. Why did they bring Tertullus?
3. What did Paul own he had said?
4. Why did not Felix release Paul?
5. What great pleasure did he allow Paul to have?

LV.

1. Who was Drusilla?
2. While Paul was speaking of Christ, how did Felix feel?
3. Did Felix send for him again?
4. Why did he leave him in prison when he went away?

LVI.

1. Who was the next governor?
2. Where did he hear of Paul?
3. What did the Jews want him to do?
4. Did Festus consent?
5. When was Paul judged by Festus?
6. Where did Paul say he wished to go to be judged?

LVII.

1. Who came to see Festus?
2. Who told him of Paul?
3. Why did Festus say Paul was mad?
4. What did Agrippa say to Paul?
5. How did Paul answer him?

LVIII.

1. Under whose care was Paul placed in the ship?
2. What two friends went with him?
3. Were there any other prisoners besides Paul?
4. Where did the ship first stop?
5. Why did Paul change from his first ship?
6. Why did this ship sail slowly?
7. What did Paul tell the ship's company would happen if they did not stop at the Fair Havens, where they were?

LIX.

1. After they set sail, what change took place in the wind?
2. How did the sailors keep the ship together?
3. How did they lighten the ship?
4. How did Paul know he should not be lost?
5. What had they not seen for a long time?
6. What did Paul say they ought to have done?
7. How did he know no one would be lost?

LX.

1. Why did the sailors let down the plummet?
2. Why did they cast four anchors?
3. What plans did the sailors make to escape?
4. Who prevented their escape?
5. And how?
6. How long had they all been without eating a meal?
7. Who encouraged them to eat?
8. How many were on board?

LXI.

1. When day dawned, what did they all see?
2. How did they try to get into the creek?
3. What hindered them?
4. What broke the ship?
5. What did the soldiers wish to do?
6. Who would not consent?
7. How did they all get to land?

LXII.

1. On what island were they cast?
2. Who were the inhabitants?
3. How did they treat the shipwrecked people?
4. How did Paul help the rest?
5. What sprung out of the fire?
6. Why did the barbarians think Paul was a god?

LXIII.

1. Who invited Paul to his house?
2. What good did Paul do to his family?
3. Why did every one want to have Paul?
4. How long did the ship's company stay there?
5. How did they get away?
6. Where did they land?
7. What favour did the centurion grant Paul?
8. How did Paul go to Rome?
9. What cheered him on the way?

LXIV.

1. Where was he allowed to live in Rome?
2. Whom did Paul invite to see him?
3. Why did Paul ask them to come again?
4. Did the Jews believe?
5. How long did Paul continue in his lodging in Rome?

LXV.

1. Who confessed his sin to Paul?
2. What was the name of his master?
3. What did Paul do for Onesimus?
4. What other visitor had Paul?
5. What advice did Paul give the children?
6. Did Paul write to any whom he had not seen?
7. Who took this letter?
8. From which of the Churches did Paul receive a present?

9. Who brought the present?
10. What did Paul earnestly ask from God?
11. Was his prayer heard?
12. Who was dear to Paul as a son?
13. What made Paul's second imprisonment **very** sad?
14. How did Paul die?

LXVI.

1. Where was John sent in his old age?
2. By whom?
3. Whom did he once see there?
4. What was he told to write?
5. To whom was the first letter?
6. What were they blamed for?
7. What did John *first* see in Heaven?
8. What terrible sights did he behold?
9. Like what did Jesus come?
10. What was done to Satan?
11. What became of the righteous dead?
12. What became of the wicked dead?
13. What did John see come down from **Heaven?**
14. Who showed him these things?
15. What did Jesus say of liars?
16. What did Jesus say of Himself?
17. What was John's last prayer?

Works by the same Author.

NURSERY BIBLE SERIES.
In the following Order. First for 4, the last for 10 years of age.

I.

THE PEEP OF DAY;
OR,
A SERIES OF THE EARLIEST RELIGIOUS INSTRUCTION THE INFANT MIND IS CAPABLE OF RECEIVING.

18mo. with 27 Illust. Cloth, 2s.; roxb. 2s.6d. School Edition, 1s. 2d. LARGE EDIT. Sq. cr. 8vo. with 11 full-page Illus. in colours, cl. 3s. 6d. Popular Edition, with 24 Illustrations, 18mo. cloth, 6d.

OVER 600,000 copies of this Book (published originally in 1833) have been sold in England at 2s. and 1s. 2d. There have been editions printed and sold by thousands in America; and the Work has been translated and published in French, German, Russian, Samoan, Chinese, and many other languages, both for Missionary and general Educational use.

The Indian Government, in their Educational Report for April, 1873, specially recommended the Work for use in their Mission-schools; and Missionaries have testified to the fact that by having the Book in English, and translating it verbatim, they have been enabled to bring the truths of the Bible within the comprehension and home to the hearts of the heathen when their own explanations have failed.

Works by the same Author.

2.
STREAKS OF LIGHT;
Or, FIFTY-TWO FACTS FROM THE BIBLE.
64th Thousand. 52 Illust. 18mo. cloth, 2s. 6d.; roxb. 3s.
Cheap Edition, Illustrated, limp cloth, 1s. 6d.

3.
LINE UPON LINE;
Or, A SECOND SERIES OF RELIGIOUS INSTRUCTION.
Part I. 355th Thous. Ques. & 30 Illust. 18mo. cl. 2s. 6d.; roxb. 3s.
Part II. 269th Thous. Ques. & 27 Illust. 18mo. cl. 2s. 6d.; roxb. 3s.
Cheap Edition, Illustrated, limp cloth, each, 1s. 4d.
Popular Edition ,,   ,,   ,,   9d.

4.
PRECEPT UPON PRECEPT.
56th Thous. Ques. 68 Illust. & Map. 18mo. cloth, 2s. 6d.; roxb. 3s.
Cheap Edition, Illustrated, limp cloth, 1s. 6d.

5.
APOSTLES PREACHING to Jews & Gentiles;
Or, THE ACTS EXPLAINED TO CHILDREN.
21st Thous. Questions. 27 Illust. & Map. 18mo. cl. 2s. 6d.; roxb. 3s.
Cheap Edition, Illustrated, limp cloth, 1s. 4d.

6.
LINES LEFT OUT.
59th Thousand. Questions & 28 Illust. 18mo. cloth, 2s. 6d.; roxb. 3s.
Cheap Edition, Illustrated, limp cloth, 1s. 6d.

7.
THE KINGS OF ISRAEL AND JUDAH.
28th Thous. 27 Illust. and Map. 18mo. cloth, 2s. 6d.; roxb. 3s.
Cheap Edition, Illustrated, limp cloth, 1s. 6d.

8.
THE CAPTIVITY OF JUDAH.
With Ques. 13th Thous. 27 Illust. & Map. 18mo. cl. 2s. 6d.; roxb. 3s.
Cheap Edition, Illustrated, limp cloth, 1s. 6d.

9.
MORE ABOUT JESUS.
With Ques. 65th Thous. 26 Illust. 18mo. cloth, 2s. 6d.; roxb. 3s.
Cheap Edition, Illustrated, limp cloth, 1s. 4d.

10.
The above Series in a Handsome Nursery Box.
10 vols. roxb. gilt edges, 31s. 6d.
Cheap School Series. 10 vols. leatherette, 21s.

Works by the same Author.

GEOGRAPHIES FOR CHILDREN (11, 12, AND 13).

11.
NEAR HOME;
Or, Europe Described to Children. With Anecdotes.
New Edition (92nd Thous.), carefully revised. Crown 8vo. 5s.
With 22 full-page and 79 smaller Illust. (50 new) and Coloured Map.

12
FAR OFF. Part I.
Or, Asia Described. With Anecdotes.
New Edition (51st Thous.). 516 pp. carefully revised. Crown 8vo. 5s.
With 95 small and 16 full-page, and 2 Col. Illust. and Col. Map.

13.
FAR OFF. Part II.
Or, Oceania, Africa, and America Described.
New Edition (39th Thous.). 520 pp. carefully revised. Crown 8vo. 5s.
With over 200 Illust. and Col. Map.

14.
LATIN WITHOUT TEARS;
Or, One Word a Day. Sq. 16mo. cloth, 3s. 6d.

15.
READING WITHOUT TEARS;
A Pleasant Mode of Learning to Read.
Part I. 69th Thous. 520 Illustrations. 16mo. *large type*, 2s. 6d.
Part II. 35th Thous. 130 Illustrations. 16mo. *large type*, 2s. 6d.
Complete in One Volume, Illustrated, 16mo. cloth extra, 4s. 6d.

16.
READING DISENTANGLED.
A Series of Classified Lessons, in 37 Sheets. 21st Edition.
Plain, 4s. the set; Mounted for Hanging, 7s.
Coloured in Sheets, 7s.; Mounted, 10s. 6d.

Works by the same Author.

17.
LIGHT IN THE DWELLING;
Or, A Harmony of the Four Gospels.

With very short and simple Remarks adapted to Family Reading, and arranged in 365 Sections for every day of the year.

28th Thousand. Thick crown 8vo. cloth, 6s.; calf, 14s.; mor. 17s. 6d.

18.
THE NIGHT OF TOIL;
Or, First Missionary Labours in the South-Sea Islands.

Seventh and Cheaper Edition, with 9 Illust. Fcap. 8vo. cloth, 3s. 6d.

19.
TEACHING MYSELF;
Or, An Abridgment of 'Reading Without Tears.'
For the Cottager.

21st Thousand. 92 Illustrations. Sq. 16mo. paper cover, 3d.

20.
THE ANGEL'S MESSAGE;
Or, The Saviour Made Known to the Cottager.

22nd Thousand. With 9 Illustrations. Sq. 16mo. paper cover, 2d.

Over 1,500,000 *Copies of this Author's Works have been sold.*

LONDON: HATCHARDS, 187 PICCADILLY.

www.ingramcontent.com/pod-product-compliance
Lightning Source LLC
Chambersburg PA
CBHW031426230426
43668CB00007B/458